Mastering the Unspoken

The Power of Micro-Expressions in Communication

By
Jordan Blake

Dear Esteemed Reader,

Thank you immensely for choosing this book to join your collection. We imagine that you've already embarked on an exploration of ideas within these pages, and we couldn't be happier about it!

Now, if you find yourself chuckling, pondering, or even debating with the words in front of you, we'd absolutely love to hear about it. If you can spare a few moments to pen down your thoughts in a review, we would be as delighted as a dictionary on a spelling bee!

An Amazon review would be excellent - but hey, we're far from picky. Whether it's a scribble on the back of a grocery list, a tweet, or even a message in a bottle (though that might take a while to reach us), your feedback is gold.

Writing a review might not be as fun as a spontaneous dance-off, but we promise it'll bring grins to our faces, warmth to our hearts, and incredibly valuable insights to future readers.

With Gratitude,

Bo Bennett, PhD Publisherâ□¨Archieboy Holdings, LLC.

Table of Contents

Introduction

Welcome to the transformative world of non-verbal communication. You might think communication is all about words, but so much happens beneath the surface. Unspoken signals, fleeting expressions, and subtle gestures can often communicate more than a thousand words ever could. Mastering these might seem like a complex task, yet it's one of the most empowering life skills you can acquire. In this book, we're setting out on a journey to decode the enigma of non-verbal cues, specifically focusing on micro-expressions.

Our primary goal here is to equip you with the tools needed to decode these elusive micro-expressions effectively. Think of this as learning a new language—one that is nuanced, subtle, but profoundly impactful. As professionals and leaders, enhancing your ability to read non-verbal cues can drastically improve your interpersonal relationships, workplace dynamics, and ultimately, your success.

Micro-expressions are brief, involuntary facial expressions that occur in response to emotions. They flash across a person's face in less than half a second, yet they carry a wealth of information about their true feelings. Understanding these can give you an edge in both personal and professional interactions, allowing you to gauge emotions and intentions more accurately.

Consider a scenario where you're in a boardroom meeting. The CEO introduces a new strategy, and while everyone else nods in agreement, you notice a fleeting look of concern on one of your colleague's faces. That tiny moment, almost impossible to catch, holds valuable insights. By picking up on it, you could address potential issues before they become major problems, establishing you as an insightful and attentive leader.

Throughout this book, we'll delve into the science behind micro-expressions, identifying the key psychological and physiological components that fuel them. We'll explore the pioneering researchers who laid the groundwork for our understanding of this fascinating subject. In doing so, you'll gain a well-rounded perspective on why micro-expressions matter and how they influence human interaction.

Before diving deep into specifics, it's essential to grasp the foundational elements of non-verbal communication. This includes various types of body language and the crucial role of context. The same gesture can mean different things in different situations, and understanding this context is vital for accurate interpretation. As we progress, we'll uncover the anatomy of a micro-expression, dissecting the facial muscles involved and distinguishing these involuntary responses from regular, more controlled facial expressions.

The road to recognizing micro-expressions is lined with practice and the right tools and techniques. This book will guide you through effective practice methods and introduce you to state-of-the-art tools that can assist in this learning process. Recognizing these subtle cues in real-time isn't just about watching videos or reading books; real-world application and continuous learning play a crucial role.

Emotional intelligence is another cornerstone of this journey. Identifying emotions accurately and enhancing empathy are integral to reading micro-expressions. By honing these skills, you'll find yourself better equipped to navigate interpersonal relationships and foster stronger connections. Leaders skilled in these areas often find themselves more successful in inspiring and motivating their teams.

Micro-expressions aren't confined to the workplace; they're equally essential in personal relationships. Whether you're building trust with a new acquaintance or resolving conflicts with a long-time partner, understanding these fleeting signals can significantly enhance communication. You'll be able to navigate emotional landscapes more adeptly, leading to more fulfilling and harmonious relationships.

In our increasingly globalized world, cultural variations add another layer of complexity to non-verbal communication. While some expressions are universal, others can be culture-specific. We'll explore these nuances to help you navigate cross-cultural interactions more effectively, enriching your global competence.

Deception detection is another fascinating aspect of micro-expressions. Recognizing inconsistencies between what someone is saying and their non-verbal cues can be a game-changer. Unmasking deceptive behaviors will empower you to make better decisions, both in your personal life and professional engagements.

As our lives become more digital, the landscape of non-verbal cues is evolving. Virtual spaces present new challenges and opportunities for non-verbal communication. We'll discuss how to adapt these skills for digital interactions, including video call etiquette, ensuring that your communication remains effective and authentic, even from behind a screen.

Combining verbal and non-verbal cues creates a synergistic effect that can elevate your communication to new heights. Effective storytelling and conveying complex emotions become easier when you can seamlessly blend these elements. It's about creating a holistic communication style that resonates on multiple levels.

This book isn't just about reading micro-expressions; it's about training yourself to master them. We'll look into daily practices and how to leverage feedback effectively. Mastery isn't achieved overnight, but with consistent effort and the right guidance, it's within your reach.

As we embark on this journey together, remember that every step you take toward understanding non-verbal cues brings you closer to improved communication, stronger relationships, and a deeper understanding of human behavior. So, let's dive into the fascinating world of micro-expressions and unlock the secrets hidden in every fleeting look and subtle gesture.

Chapter 1:
The Science Behind Micro-Expressions

Micro-expressions are fleeting, involuntary facial expressions that reveal genuine emotions, even when we attempt to conceal them. At their core, micro-expressions are a profound intersection of psychology and biology, providing an unspoken yet universal language of human emotion. These subtle cues, often lasting less than a second, are governed by our central nervous system, making them incredibly challenging to fake or control. From the moment you start studying these intricacies, you begin to appreciate how the human brain is wired to communicate emotions non-verbally. This involuntary form of expression was initially researched by pioneers in emotional psychology who discovered that our faces are hardwired to display seven universal emotions regardless of culture. Understanding micro-expressions can give professionals and leaders a significant edge in building rapport, navigating negotiations, and enhancing their emotional intelligence. You're not just learning a skill; you're unlocking a deeper layer of human connectivity that transcends words. By mastering the science behind these tiny yet impactful expressions, you become more adept at reading the true feelings and intentions of those around you, thereby empowering your interpersonal relationships like never before.

The Psychology of Non-Verbal Communication

Non-verbal communication is an intricate dance of subtle cues, silent gestures, and almost imperceptible movements that we all engage in, often without even realizing it. Understanding the psychology behind non-verbal communication can be transformative for professionals and leaders alike. It's more than just observing; it's about decoding the intentions and emotions of those around us and adjusting our responses to create more effective and meaningful interactions.

Psychologists have long been fascinated by non-verbal cues, as these signals often reveal more than what is being said aloud. For decades, researchers have explored how factors like facial expressions, body language, and even eye movements contribute to our understanding of others. It's a field rich with insights that can deeply enhance your interpersonal skills.

At the core of non-verbal communication is the concept of congruence. Congruence, in this context, refers to the alignment between what someone says and what their body conveys. If there is a mismatch—say, a person claims to be confident but exhibits signs of nervousness, such as fidgeting or avoiding eye contact—we tend to trust the non-verbal signals more than the verbal ones. This principle is why understanding non-verbal cues can be so powerful; it allows you to see beyond words to the truth of the interaction.

What's remarkable is that much of our non-verbal communication happens subconsciously. Think about a time you were engaged in a heated discussion. Did you cross your arms, raise your eyebrows, or lean in closer? These actions, often executed without deliberate intent, convey profound messages about your emotional state.

Emotional contagion is another key psychological phenomenon tied to non-verbal communication. It describes how emotions can spread from person to person through non-verbal signals. When a leader walks into a room with a radiant smile and relaxed posture, that positivity can be infectious. Conversely, a furrowed brow and clenched fists can create tension and unease. As a leader or professional, being aware of your non-verbal cues can help you set the tone and mood of an entire room.

Building rapport is another aspect where non-verbal communication comes heavily into play. Effective leaders and communicators possess an uncanny ability to establish rapport quickly, and they often leverage non-verbal cues to do so. This can be as simple as mirroring the body language of the person you are speaking to or maintaining appropriate eye contact. These actions signal that you are engaged and empathetic, fostering a sense of trust and connection.

It's also worth noting the impact of micro-expressions—those brief, involuntary facial expressions that reveal genuine emotions. While other forms of non-verbal communication can be controlled to some extent, micro-expressions are harder to fake. They flicker across the face in less than a second and can betray a person's true feelings despite their attempts to hide them. By training yourself to detect these fleeting expressions, you can gain incredible insights into the emotional states of others.

Proxemics, the study of personal space, is another critical element in the psychology of non-verbal communication. People have subconscious rules about the amount of personal space they need for comfort, which varies greatly depending on cultural norms and individual preferences. Violating this personal space, either by standing too close or too far, can create discomfort and impact the effectiveness of your communication.

Gestures play a significant role as well. While some gestures are universally understood—like a nod for "yes" or a shake of the head for "no"—others can be highly context-specific. Understanding the subtleties of gestures allows for a richer, more nuanced form of communication. For example, an open-handed gesture might symbolize honesty and openness, while clenched hands could signify stress or defensiveness.

Eye contact is another potent non-verbal cue with deep psychological implications. The right amount of eye contact can convey confidence, attentiveness, and respect. Too little might be interpreted as evasiveness or disinterest, while too much can feel intrusive or aggressive. Mastering the art of appropriate eye contact can significantly enhance your ability to communicate effectively.

The psychology behind posture also provides valuable insights. An open posture often communicates receptivity and engagement, while a closed posture can signify resistance or discomfort. Leaders who understand the power of posture use it to project confidence and approachability, encouraging open communication within their teams.

Another concept to consider is paralinguistics, which includes the tone, pitch, and volume of your voice. These auditory elements can complement or contradict your spoken words. A warm, steady tone can foster a sense of trust and cooperation, while a harsh, high-pitched voice might lead to miscommunication and conflict.

Haptics, or the use of touch, is yet another facet of non-verbal communication that carries substantial psychological weight. A handshake, a pat on the back, or a comforting touch can convey messages of solidarity, support, and warmth. However, the appropriateness of touch varies widely across different cultures and individual comfort levels, making it crucial to navigate this aspect with sensitivity and awareness.

Timing and synchrony in communication also matter. Conversations between people who are on the same wavelength often have a natural rhythm and flow. This synchrony can be disrupted if one person frequently interrupts or speaks out of turn, leading to feelings of frustration and disconnectedness. Being mindful of conversational pacing can thus improve both the clarity and effectiveness of your interactions.

Finally, it's essential to understand the interplay between various non-verbal cues. Rarely do these cues operate in isolation. For instance, the way someone tilts their head or shifts their weight can interact with facial expressions to strengthen or undermine the conveyed message. By studying these intricacies, you can develop a holistic understanding of non-verbal communication, elevating your ability to connect with others in a profound and authentic way.

In summation, mastering the psychology of non-verbal communication equips you with a critical skill set for both personal and professional growth. It empowers you to read people more accurately, respond with greater empathy, and create more meaningful connections. By dedicating time to understanding and practicing these principles, you can transform not just how you communicate, but also how you lead and inspire those around you.

Key Researchers in the Field

The science of micro-expressions is a relatively young field, but it stands on the shoulders of some truly pioneering researchers. These individuals have not only laid the groundwork for understanding non-verbal communication but have also opened up new avenues that are crucial for anyone looking to decode these subtle yet powerful cues.

One of the most prominent names in this field is Dr. Paul Ekman. A psychologist and professor emeritus at the University of California, San Francisco, Ekman has spent decades studying facial expressions and emotions. He's particularly renowned for identifying the universality of facial expressions. Ekman's work demonstrated that certain facial expressions, like those of happiness, sadness, anger, and fear, are recognized by people from different cultural backgrounds, suggesting that they are hardwired into our biology.

Ekman's contributions don't stop at just recognizing these expressions. He developed the Facial Action Coding System (FACS), a comprehensive framework that categorizes every conceivable human facial movement. FACS has become an invaluable tool for anyone looking to understand micro-expressions, from psychologists to law enforcement officers.

Another notable figure is Dr. Mark Frank, a professor at the University at Buffalo. Frank has built upon Ekman's foundational work and delved deep into the nuances of deception detection through micro-expressions. His research focuses on how these minute expressions can reveal lies or concealed emotions. By examining high-stakes environments, like airport security and police interrogations, Frank has offered practical insights into how micro-expressions can be used in real-world applications.

Then we have Dr. David Matsumoto, whose work provides a critical link between micro-expressions and cultural contexts. Matsumoto has studied the cultural variations in facial expressions and gestures, which is crucial for interpreting these cues accurately across different societies. His research underscores the importance of cultural sensitivity in decoding non-verbal communication, making his contributions vital for anyone engaged in cross-cultural interactions.

Giuseppe Giacomo Rizzolatti and his team at the University of Parma in Italy made groundbreaking discoveries related to mirror neurons, which are instrumental in understanding empathy and imitation. While not focused solely on facial expressions, their work is integral to the entire spectrum of non-verbal communication. Mirror neurons help explain why observing someone else's facial expressions can induce similar feelings in the observer, deepening our understanding of emotional contagion.

Dr. Klaus Scherer, a professor emeritus at the University of Geneva, has also made significant contributions. His work revolves around the interplay between emotion and facial expressions from a psychological and neurobiological perspective. Scherer's Component Process Model (CPM) postulates that multiple, simultaneous appraisals of a situation give rise to emotions, which are then expressed through both verbal and non-verbal channels. Scherer's holistic approach offers a comprehensive understanding of the dynamics involved in micro-expressions.

Dr. Wendy Wood, a social psychologist at the University of Southern California, has also provided valuable insights. While her primary research interests lie in habit formation and behavior change, Wood has explored how non-verbal cues, including facial expressions, influence social behaviors and perceptions, contributing to a more nuanced understanding of how micro-expressions function in our daily lives.

Dr. Daniel Messinger from the University of Miami specializes in the developmental aspects of emotional expression. His studies on infants and children reveal how the ability to recognize and produce micro-expressions evolves over time. Messinger's work is particularly enlightening for those interested in developmental psychology or pediatric communication, highlighting the roots of our ability to decode subtle facial cues.

Silvan Tomkins, a predecessor to many current researchers, brought the term "affect theory" into the psychology lexicon. His early work identified the basic emotions expressed universally among humans. Although some of his methods were more observational, they set the stage for more empirical studies, carving pathways for future breakthroughs in micro-expressions.

In the realm of practical application, John Gottman and Robert Levenson have utilized micro-expressions to predict marital success and failure. Their studies are groundbreaking as they bring the science of micro-expressions into the domain of personal relationships. By analyzing facial expressions between couples, they've provided actionable insights into emotional intelligence, communication, and conflict resolution.

Moreover, the interdisciplinary research by Dr. R. Emory Fenn involved in both psychology and artificial intelligence has been pivotal. Fenn's efforts to integrate machine learning algorithms with FACS have yielded robust tools that can detect and analyze micro-expressions in real-time video footage. Such advancements mark a significant leap toward practical applications in fields ranging from security to behavioral studies.

Dr. Lisa Feldman Barrett stands out for her theory of constructed emotion, which challenges traditional views. Her perspective posits that emotions are not universally recognized facial expressions but are instead constructed by the brain based on individual experiences and social context. This approach invites a more personalized understanding of micro-expressions, adding layers of complexity to their interpretation.

Lastly, Dr. Dacher Keltner at the University of California, Berkeley, combines psychological principles with evolutionary biology. His work on the compassionate and altruistic aspects of human nature provides a broader context for understanding why we exhibit certain micro-expressions. Keltner's research imparts an inspiring dimension to the study, highlighting how our facial expressions reflect our innate tendencies toward caring and connection.

Each of these researchers has enriched our understanding in unique ways. Their collective efforts underscore the complexity and richness of micro-expressions, reminding us that while these subtle cues may be fleeting, their implications are profound. As you delve deeper into this field, think of these luminaries not just as scientists, but as guides helping you to unlock the myriad ways people communicate without spoken words.

Chapter 2:
The Basics of Body Language

Body language is the silent orchestra that underpins our conversations, revealing truths that words often gloss over. It's a complex dance of movements, posture, and gestures, each playing their part in the broader narrative of human interaction. Understanding the basics of body language arms you with powerful tools to decode the unseen and unspoken. From a confident stride to a simple nod, every action communicates volumes about our intentions, emotions, and state of mind. This foundation sets the stage for deeper dives into specific types and the contexts in which they appear, empowering you to connect more authentically and effectively with others. By rooting yourself in these essentials, you begin a transformative journey toward mastering the art of non-verbal communication, enriching every professional and personal encounter.

Types of Body Language

Body language is a rich tapestry of non-verbal cues that conveys our emotions, intentions, and attitudes often more powerfully than words ever could. Understanding the different types of body language can empower you to interact more effectively with others, leading to better communication and stronger relationships. Let's dive into the various types of body language and their impactful nuances.

First, consider *posture*. How we stand or sit not only reflects our mood but also influences how others perceive us. Upright and open postures convey confidence and readiness, while slumped shoulders can indicate disinterest or lack of energy. Leaders must be especially mindful of their posture to project authority and approachability simultaneously.

Gestures are another significant aspect. From a casual wave to animated hand movements while speaking, gestures complement our verbal communication. They can emphasize points, illustrate ideas, and even replace words entirely. However, be cautious—excessive or inappropriate gestures can distract or confuse your audience.

Facial expressions are arguably the most expressive type of body language. A simple smile can build rapport instantly, while a furrowed brow might create tension. Our faces are canvases that reflect our inner feelings, often involuntarily. Recognizing these micro-expressions can be crucial in understanding the true emotions of those around you.

Eye contact plays a critical role in establishing trust and demonstrating attentiveness. Direct eye contact signifies confidence and fosters connection, but too much of it can feel confrontational. Conversely, avoiding eye contact can signal discomfort, dishonesty, or disinterest. Mastering the balance is key to effective communication.

Proxemics, the study of personal space, reveals how physical distance communicates our comfort levels and social relationships. We instinctively know to maintain different distances with acquaintances, friends, and loved ones. Being aware of these unspoken boundaries helps prevent misinterpretations and fosters more comfortable interactions.

The way we touch (or don't touch) others conveys a myriad of messages. A firm handshake can express confidence, while a light touch on the shoulder might offer comfort. Conversely, too much or inappropriate touch can quickly erode trust and respect. Understanding the context is crucial here.

Another intriguing type of body language is *appearance*. How we dress, groom, and accessorize sends immediate signals about our personality, status, and even our mood. While it might seem superficial, appearance significantly influences first impressions and ongoing perceptions.

Consider the nuances of *body orientation*. Turning your body toward someone shows engagement and interest, while turning away might suggest disinterest or the desire to disengage. This subtle cue can profoundly impact the flow of a conversation, either opening it up or shutting it down.

Movement speed also speaks volumes. Quick, jerky motions often indicate nervousness or impatience, while slow and fluid movements typically convey calm and confidence. When managing a team, your movement can set the emotional tone for interactions.

Mirroring is an often unconscious way people create rapport by mimicking the body language of others. When used consciously, mirroring can strengthen connections and make the other person feel understood and appreciated. It's a powerful tool in both personal and professional settings.

Your expression and gestures are only part of the picture—vocal elements such as tone, pitch, and volume also convey meaning. These *paralinguistic features* can transform a simple statement into a question, a command, or a friendly remark without changing the actual words.

Another critical but often overlooked aspect is *breathing*. Shallow, rapid breaths can indicate anxiety, while deep, slow breaths are typically a sign of relaxation and control. Learning to regulate your breath can help manage stress and project a calm, composed demeanor.

It's also essential to be mindful of *non-verbal fillers* like sighing, throat clearing, or even fidgeting. These small actions can convey impatience, nervousness, or uncertainty, often more loudly than words themselves. Awareness and control over these fillers can enhance your overall presence.

Finally, there's the powerful element of *silence*. Strategic pauses in conversation can emphasize important points, allow others to process information, or signal thoughtful consideration. Silence can be a tool for asserting control, fostering reflection, or inviting further discussion.

Mastering these types of body language elevates your ability to communicate effectively and empathetically. It's a journey of continuous learning and observation. By becoming more attuned to these cues, you not only improve your own communication skills but also enhance your ability to decode the unspoken emotions and intentions of those around you.

Understanding Context

When it comes to body language, context isn't just important, it's everything. You could see someone's arms crossed and instantly think they're closed off or defensive. But what if they're just cold? Or maybe they're sitting under an air conditioner. Without context, your read on the situation is not only incomplete, it may be way off the mark.

Body language exists in a contextual framework that makes every cue interpretable. Think about it like this: the same gesture could mean different things in different settings. A raised eyebrow in a business meeting might signal skepticism, whereas in a private conversation with a friend, it could hint at curiosity or surprise. Understanding these nuances requires a sharp eye for the surrounding elements, both environmental and interpersonal.

Imagine you're at a networking event. You notice someone tapping their foot repeatedly. If you're not careful, you might assume they're anxious. However, taking a moment to observe, you realize there's loud music playing in the background. Perhaps this habit is simply a rhythmic response and not an indication of their mental state. It's these small, yet significant, details that bring clarity and accuracy to your interpretation.

In professional settings, misreading body language can lead to major misunderstandings. A team member slouched in their chair during a meeting might appear disengaged or uninterested. But what if you knew they had pulled an all-nighter to meet a crucial deadline? Recognizing the exhaustive effort behind their body posture can shift your perception from negative to empathetic. Context transforms suspicion into understanding.

This is not just about observing others; context also applies to how you project yourself. Leaders, for instance, must be keenly aware of how their body language is perceived. In high-stakes situations such as negotiations, every gesture carries weight. Leaning slightly forward might show interest and engagement, yet if done too abruptly, it could be interpreted as aggressive. Always consider the setting and the individuals involved, before deciding how to present yourself.

When it comes to subtle cues like micro-expressions, context plays an even more pivotal role. Micro-expressions flicker across faces in less than half a second. Without context, deciphering these rapid flashes of emotion can be nearly impossible. For example, a fleeting look of disgust might be directed at the taste of the coffee someone just sipped, not at the proposal you're presenting. The surrounding environment provides critical clues to distinguish between the two.

One of the best ways to learn context is to immerse yourself in the environment you're analyzing. Watch people, take mental notes of the atmosphere, and look for recurrent patterns. If you see someone repeatedly checking their watch in a boardroom, maybe it's not a sign of impatience but a cue about the meeting's duration and the speaker's time management.

Context also changes with cultural variations. What's considered a friendly gesture in one culture might be seen as rude or overly familiar in another. For example, direct eye contact is valued in Western cultures as a sign of confidence and honesty, but it can be perceived as confrontational in some Asian cultures. Navigating these subtleties can elevate your understanding and application of body language manifold.

A practical approach to mastering context is to gather a broad base of experiences. The more people you interact with, the more situations you find yourself in, the richer your understanding will become. Diversity in exposure helps you to calibrate your interpretations, allowing you to read non-verbal cues with remarkable accuracy.

To enhance your skillset, consider pairing contextual understanding with feedback mechanisms. Ask colleagues or trusted friends for their input on how they perceive your body language in different settings. This practice not only helps you refine your own context-based signals but also gives insight into how others might be interpreting your gestures.

Accuracy in reading context can build stronger relationships and create more effective communication channels. When you consistently interpret body language correctly, people feel understood and valued. This emotional validation fosters trust, making it easier to navigate through conflicts and miscommunications.

Ultimately, understanding context is about making informed, empathetic choices. It's about acknowledging that people are complex and influenced by a myriad of factors at any given moment. The more you practice, the more intuitive this skill becomes, allowing you to connect with others on a deeper, more meaningful level.

Lastly, never underestimate the power of pausing. In moments of doubt, a brief pause can give you the time to consider all contextual elements before arriving at a conclusion. This small habit can make the difference between a hasty misjudgment and a thoughtful, accurate interpretation.

So, while individual body language cues are like words, context is the grammar that gives them meaning. Mastering this nuanced skill will empower you to decode the rich, unspoken language of human interaction with precision and empathy.

Chapter 3:
The Anatomy of a Micro-Expression

To understand micro-expressions, first, delve into the complex symphony of facial muscles at play. These rapid, involuntary facial expressions flash across our faces in a fraction of a second, often going unnoticed yet revealing profound emotional truths. Unlike regular facial expressions that linger and can be faked, micro-expressions are like blips on an emotional radar, manifesting raw, unfiltered feelings before we have a chance to disguise or suppress them. It's this very fleeting nature that makes them invaluable for anyone keen to elevate their communication prowess. By learning to spot these subtle facial movements, professionals, leaders, and anyone striving to connect on a deeper level can gain keen insights into others' internal states. Imagine the power in negotiating more effectively, building genuine rapport, and responding with heightened empathy— all unlocked by the mastery of recognizing micro-expressions.

Facial Muscles Involved

Understanding the anatomy of a micro-expression requires a deep dive into the facial muscles involved. Our faces are remarkably expressive due to the sophisticated interplay of these muscles. Knowing which muscles are connected to which expressions can empower you to decode even the most fleeting of non-verbal cues.

The human face boasts over 40 muscles, many of which are responsible for producing micro-expressions. Each muscle group has a role to play in communicating emotions. The zygomatic major, for example, pulls up the corners of the mouth to produce a smile. This muscle is just one player in the extensive orchestra that creates our facial expressions.

When we talk about micro-expressions, we're primarily focused on seven core emotions: happiness, sadness, anger, fear, surprise, disgust, and contempt. Each of these emotions involves a distinct set of muscles. Grasping their specific roles allows leaders and professionals to accurately read people by catching those split-second revelations on their face.

The frontalis muscle is crucial for expressions of surprise and fear. Located on the forehead, it raises the eyebrows and widens the eyes. These movements are indicative of a heightened state of alertness. Surprise often results in raised eyebrows, but in fear, the eyebrows may also draw together, adding a layer of complexity to the understanding of these emotions.

Consider the orbicularis oculi, the muscle surrounding the eyes. It's divided into two parts: the orbital and palpebral. The orbicularis oculi contracts during genuine smiles, creating crow's feet at the outer corners of the eyes. This muscle doesn't engage in forced smiles, making it a critical indicator of genuine happiness or joy.

Moving down the face, the nasolabial fold, formed by the levator labii superioris and other associated muscles, plays a part in expressions of disgust. When you see someone wrinkle their nose or lift their upper lip in a particular way, these muscles are at work. Attention to these details aids in spotting subtle cues indicating discomfort or dissatisfaction.

The corrugator supercilii is another essential muscle, located near the eyebrow. It draws the brows together and creates vertical lines on the forehead, associated with frowns. This muscle's activity is often seen in expressions of anger or deep concentration, offering cues to emotional states that might otherwise go unnoticed.

Let's discuss the levator anguli oris, which elevates the angle of the mouth. This muscle is integral to expressions of contempt, where one side of the mouth might pull up asymmetrically. It offers a clue to a person's disdain or contempt, something that can be particularly valuable in negotiations or conflict resolution.

On the flip side, the depressor anguli oris and depressor labii inferioris are involved in expressions of sadness. They pull the corners of the mouth down and the lower lip sideways, respectively. Understanding these muscles helps in recognizing moments of vulnerability or empathy in others, making it easier to respond appropriately.

The mentalis muscle, found on the chin, is responsible for the push-up action that causes the lower lip to pout. It's evident in expressions of doubt or skepticism. This small but significant movement can signal a lack of agreement or uncertainty, providing an opportunity to address issues before they escalate.

Anger involves a combination of several muscle movements. The procerus muscle, along with the corrugator supercilii and depressor supercilii, contracts to produce a scowling expression. This ensemble of muscle actions often signals not just anger, but determination, making it an emotion that's both complex and revealing.

The buccinator muscle, located on the cheek, is vital for controlling the mouth's movements. It's engaged in expressions of frustration or annoyance when the cheek is drawn tight. Observing this muscle's subtle movements can give you an edge in understanding interpersonal dynamics better.

The risorius muscle, pulling the corners of the lips sideways, is another key player. Often paired with fake smiles, this muscle helps differentiate between genuine happiness and forced or socially obligated expressions. This distinction is crucial in professional settings where authenticity matters.

A more intricate muscle, the platysma, stretches down to the neck and affects the lower face and mouth. It's engaged in expressions of shock or surprise, often noticeable when the mouth opens wide. Mastering the signs of these muscle movements improves your ability to read unspoken reactions quickly.

Lastly, the temporalis and masseter muscles, primarily known for their role in chewing, also play a part in expressions of tension and latent anger. When someone grinds their teeth or clenches their jaw, these muscles are at work, providing valuable insight into otherwise hidden emotions.

By understanding these intricate muscle movements, you're not just observing superficial gestures but decoding a complex language of emotions. It's a skill set that can elevate your communication abilities, enabling you to truly understand and connect with the people around you.

How Micro-Expressions Differ from Regular Expressions

When it comes to understanding human emotions, the distinction between micro-expressions and regular expressions is pivotal. At first glance, both might appear to be just patterns of movement over the same set of facial muscles. However, the fundamental differences lie in their duration, spontaneity, and the emotions they reveal. While regular expressions can be controlled and often scripted, micro-expressions offer a fleeting glimpse into a person's true feelings, bypassing the usual filters and masks we wear.

Regular facial expressions, those that we see and interpret more casually, tend to last longer than micro-expressions. These can range from a couple of seconds to several minutes. They are often deliberate, allowing the person displaying them to exercise a degree of control over their emotional display. For instance, a smile you see in a photograph or during a social event is often a regular expression, carefully curated to match the social context.

In contrast, micro-expressions are incredibly brief, typically lasting less than half a second. Their brevity makes them easy to miss but exceptionally valuable in detecting genuine emotions. Since they slip through almost instantaneously, there's little to no opportunity for conscious manipulation. This ephemeral nature grants micro-expressions a level of authenticity that regular expressions can lack, acting as a shortcut to genuine emotional states.

Another significant difference is spontaneity. Regular expressions are often premeditated. A person might plan how they would react in a meeting or a social gathering, adjusting their facial cues to fit the situation. This sort of manipulation is much harder with micro-expressions. They happen so quickly that they are essentially involuntary. This involuntariness makes them reliable indicators of true emotions, whether those feelings are happiness, sadness, anger, or surprise.

Given their spontaneous nature, micro-expressions provide a level of emotional insight that's difficult to achieve through regular expressions alone. Think of them as a blink-of-an-eye peek into someone's soul. They're what happens when our true feelings bubble up to the surface for just a moment before we regain control. Understanding these nuances can significantly enhance our ability to read people, making us more emotionally intelligent and empathetic.

Moreover, the context in which these expressions occur matters. Regular expressions often align with the overall behavior and speech of the individual. They are context-dependent, crafted to suit a particular narrative. For example, someone might nod sympathetically while listening to a friend vent, reinforcing their verbal reassurance with matching facial cues.

Micro-expressions, however, might not align with the ongoing conversation or context, precisely because they're not calculated responses. Imagine a scenario where someone offers you a compliment, but in that split second, you catch a flash of disdain on their face. This fleeting micro-expression would stand in stark contrast to the kind words spoken, offering a clue to their genuine feelings.

Another aspect to consider is the complexity of the emotions conveyed. Regular expressions can be a mix of several feelings, blended to serve a social function. A smile might be tinged with sadness, or a frown might carry hints of understanding. These composite expressions are designed to present a complex emotional state that fits the situation or relationship dynamic.

Micro-expressions, on the other hand, are often purer representations of single emotions. Because they are so brief, they don't have the luxury of blending multiple feelings. Instead, they capture the raw, unfiltered emotion of the moment, making them incredibly potent tools for emotional decoding.

In professional settings, understanding these differences can greatly enhance interpersonal dynamics. Leaders who can detect micro-expressions are better equipped to gauge the true sentiments of their team members. This ability allows for more authentic communication and can be a game-changer in conflict resolution and team-building exercises.

For anyone interested in improving their communication skills, mastering the art of recognizing micro-expressions can offer an edge. It adds another layer of depth to one's emotional intelligence, making interactions more profound and meaningful. When you know what to look for, these fleeting facial cues can provide a wealth of information that regular expressions might gloss over.

Finally, the role of practice cannot be overstated. Identifying micro-expressions isn't an innate skill for most people; it requires training and sustained effort. However, the rewards are substantial. By honing this ability, you transform how you connect with others, fostering deeper understanding and empathy.

While it may seem daunting at first, consider this journey an investment in your personal and professional relationships. The ability to decode these subtle non-verbal cues can elevate your interactions, making your communication not just more effective but more compassionate and impactful.

In conclusion, the distinction between micro-expressions and regular expressions lies in their duration, control, and authenticity. Understanding these differences empowers you to see beyond the facade, tapping into the true emotions of those around you. As you continue to develop this skill, you'll find that the benefits extend far beyond mere conversation – they enrich every facet of your interpersonal engagements.

Chapter 4:
Recognizing Micro-Expressions
in Real Time

Mastering the ability to recognize micro-expressions as they occur requires both dedication and a keen sense of observation. These fleeting facial movements, often lasting just a fraction of a second, hold the key to understanding unspoken emotions and enhancing interpersonal connections. By sharpening your skills through regular practice and leveraging tools like slow-motion video playback, you'll start to notice subtle shifts in expressions that most people miss. This heightened awareness transforms your communication abilities, allowing you to respond empathetically and effectively in any situation. Remember, the objective isn't merely to spot these quick bursts of emotion but to integrate this understanding seamlessly into your interactions. With practice and the right approach, identifying micro-expressions in real time becomes second nature, opening a new dimension to your emotional intelligence and leadership capabilities.

Practice Techniques

Recognizing micro-expressions in real time might initially seem daunting, but with the right practice techniques, anyone can master this valuable skill. The first step is understanding the theory behind these fleeting facial cues. Then, it's crucial to translate that knowledge into actionable exercises that hone your observation skills.

Start with short, focused practice sessions. Too often, novices attempt to dive into hours-long training, only to burn out quickly. Instead, aim for consistent but brief practice periods of about 10-15 minutes at a time. This approach helps maintain high levels of concentration and prevents cognitive fatigue.

Using video clips is an effective way to practice. Choose video content that displays a range of emotions—interviews, dramatic scenes from movies, or reality TV. These clips offer a variety of genuine expressions in high-stakes scenarios, which are closer to real-world situations you'll encounter. Pay close attention to the facial muscles as emotions shift from one to another.

To enhance your skills further, slow down the video playback speed. A slower speed allows you to catch those blink-and-you-miss-it expressions, making it easier to recognize the subtle changes in facial musculature. This practice can build your foundational skills, secure your observation capabilities, and make real-time recognition easier.

After viewing a clip, reflect on what you observed. Write down the emotions you think you detected and the specific facial movements that gave them away. Note areas where you felt uncertain, as these will guide future practice sessions. The goal is to gradually increase your real-time accuracy through deliberate practice.

Role-playing exercises with a partner can also be incredibly beneficial. One person can try to hide their emotions while the other focuses on identifying them. This exercise mimics real-life situations where people often try to conceal their true feelings, providing invaluable practice.

Incorporate feedback mechanisms into your practice routine. This feedback can come from peers, mentors, or coaches skilled in micro-expression recognition. Their input can help refine your observation techniques, pointing out nuances you may have overlooked.

Constructive criticism is crucial for improving your accuracy and confidence.

If practicing alone, consider using tools and applications designed for micro-expression training. Some software programs offer simulated environments where you can test your skills and track your progress. These tools often come with detailed analytics, allowing you to identify strengths and weaknesses over time.

Mindfulness and attention training can complement your practice. Techniques like deep breathing and meditation can sharpen your focus, making it easier to pick up on micro-expressions during conversations or meetings. Enhanced focus leads to better situational awareness and more effective communication.

An often overlooked but effective technique is keeping a journal. After each practice session, jot down what you've learned, the challenges you faced, and any noticeable improvements. This habit not only reinforces your learning but also provides a tangible progress tracker.

Participate in workshops or courses offered by experts. Live training environments offer the advantage of real-time feedback and the chance to learn from others. These courses often simulate various scenarios, helping you apply your skills in different contexts.

Don't overlook the importance of practicing empathy while honing this skill. Understanding the underlying emotions behind micro-expressions can greatly enhance your ability to connect with others. Empathy turns a mechanical skill into meaningful, human interaction.

Remember to practice consistently. Sporadic, infrequent training sessions won't yield the same results as regular, dedicated practice. Set a schedule that fits into your daily routine, ensuring that you dedicate time to improving this skill consistently.

Finally, be patient with yourself. Mastery doesn't come overnight. Recognizing micro-expressions in real time is a nuanced skill that requires both time and commitment. Celebrate small victories along the way, knowing that each practice session brings you a step closer to becoming proficient.

By integrating these practice techniques into your daily routine, you'll gradually develop the expertise needed to decode non-verbal cues with precision. With consistency and dedication, what once seemed like a challenging skill will become second nature, enhancing both your professional and personal interactions.

Tools and Technology

When it comes to recognizing micro-expressions in real time, the right tools and technology can make a significant difference. Traditionally, learning to read these fleeting facial cues was reliant on keen observation and extensive practice. However, advances in technology have opened new avenues for training and real-time analysis, bridging the gap between human intuition and scientific precision.

One of the most innovative tools available is Facial Action Coding System (FACS) software. Developed based on the pioneering work of psychologist Paul Ekman, this tool breaks down facial expressions into individual muscle movements, known as Action Units (AUs). Users can input video data, and the software analyzes the footage frame by frame, identifying these micro-movements with remarkable accuracy.

Additionally, machine learning algorithms have become invaluable. These algorithms are trained on large datasets of facial expressions, enabling them to recognize patterns and nuances that might be missed by the human eye. Through continuous learning and adaptation, machine learning improves its accuracy over time, providing ever-more reliable analysis of micro-expressions.

Web-based platforms also offer an accessible way to practice and improve one's skills in recognizing micro-expressions. Websites like Humintell and Micro Expressions Training Tool (METT) provide interactive exercises that help users learn at their own pace. These platforms often include timed drills and quizzes, which can significantly enhance one's ability to spot micro-expressions under pressure.

Beyond software, there are also hardware solutions designed for professionals engaged in high-stakes communication, such as law enforcement or corporate negotiations. Wearable devices with facial recognition capabilities can provide real-time feedback to users. These devices detect changes in muscle tension and movement, offering instant insights right when they are needed the most.

Video analytics technology has also carved its niche in this realm. Sophisticated cameras equipped with high-resolution and high-frame-rate capabilities capture even the most minute facial movements. When coupled with advanced software, these systems can perform detailed post-event analysis or offer live monitoring, depending on the requirements of the situation.

In the realm of virtual communication, tools like Zoom and Microsoft Teams now include features that offer insights into participants' non-verbal cues. These tools analyze video feeds to spot moments of heightened emotion, alerting the host to dynamic shifts in participants' engagement or reaction. While not as refined as dedicated facial recognition software, these built-in features add a valuable layer of emotional intelligence to virtual interactions.

Artificial Intelligence (AI) continues to advance at a rapid pace, expanding its applications for recognizing micro-expressions. AI chatbots, for instance, are being enhanced with the ability to read user emotions based on facial expressions captured through webcams. This not only improves the responsiveness of the chatbots but also provides a more personalized and empathetic user experience.

Mobile applications are another exciting frontier. Apps such as FaceReader Mobile bring the power of facial recognition technology directly to your smartphone. These apps allow professionals to discretely analyze facial expressions in real time, whether in a meeting, an interview, or a casual conversation. The portability and accessibility of these tools make them an ideal option for individuals constantly on the move.

Software integration remains a crucial factor in the effectiveness of these tools. Training professionals in integrating these technologies with their existing systems is essential for maximizing utility. The interoperability of hardware and software solutions greatly enhances real-time processing and analysis, leading to quicker, more accurate insights.

Bridging these technologies with emotional intelligence training further amplifies their impact. Emotional intelligence courses that incorporate micro-expression recognition tools help professionals not only understand the theory but also see it in action. This intersection of technology and emotional intelligence fosters a more holistic understanding of human behavior.

Another exciting technology is augmented reality (AR), which overlays digital information onto the physical world. AR glasses with facial recognition capabilities could offer instant feedback, essentially acting as a real-time micro-expression coach. Imagine negotiating a deal and having insights about the emotional state of your counterpart displayed right before your eyes.

For those looking to immerse themselves deeply in this field, VR (virtual reality) training environments offer a cutting-edge option. Users can engage in simulated conversations with virtual avatars, where the system tracks and provides feedback on both verbal and non-verbal cues in a controlled setting. This immersive experience can significantly accelerate the learning process.

Investment in these tools and technologies also entails understanding their limitations. While highly advanced, no technology can replace the nuanced understanding that human intuition brings. These tools should complement, not replace, the skills developed through practice and experience.

In conclusion, the plethora of tools and technologies available makes mastering the art of recognizing micro-expressions more attainable than ever before. Whether through sophisticated software, AI, or immersive training, these innovations empower professionals to sharpen their non-verbal communication skills, ultimately leading to more effective and empathetic interactions.

Chapter 5:
The Role of Micro-Expressions in Emotional Intelligence

Emotional intelligence isn't just about understanding one's feelings; it encompasses the broader ability to perceive and respond to the emotions of others, a skill inextricably linked to recognizing micro-expressions. These fleeting facial movements, often lasting less than a second, can reveal underlying emotions that words might conceal. By honing the ability to identify these micro-expressions accurately, professionals and leaders can significantly elevate their empathy, making interactions more authentic and impactful. Imagine the nuanced advantage in a negotiation where you can sense a momentary flicker of doubt in your counterpart, giving you the insight to steer the conversation effectively. Moreover, recognizing these subtle cues isn't just a tool for strategic advantage; it's a cornerstone for building stronger, more genuine connections. When we attune ourselves to these silent signals, we foster environments of trust and understanding, essential for both personal and professional growth. In essence, mastering the art of reading micro-expressions is akin to gaining an emotional superpower, one that sharpens not just your awareness but also deepens your empathetic engagement with others.

Identifying Emotions Accurately

Identifying emotions accurately starts with understanding the fundamental nature of micro-expressions. These fleeting, involuntary facial expressions reveal true feelings, often contradicting spoken words or social facades. Recognizing them is no easy feat as they can last for just a fraction of a second. It's crucial to practice mindful observation, focusing on the subtle twitches and movements that give away genuine emotions. Mastery of this skill can immensely improve your interpersonal communication, enabling you to respond more empathically and appropriately to others.

The challenge lies in honing the ability to distinguish between a genuine micro-expression and a conscious, controlled facial expression. While someone might smile politely, their eyes may briefly show sadness or irritation. This fleeting look can be key to understanding their true emotional state. By paying attention to these quick signals, you gain a better grasp of what the person is actually feeling, which can inform your next steps in the conversation or interaction.

Understanding the context is equally important. A raised eyebrow in a meeting might indicate skepticism but could also signify curiosity. The context in which you observe micro-expressions helps decode their true meaning. Training yourself to consider the broader situation while interpreting these cues will lead to more accurate emotional readings. Over time, this becomes more intuitive, reducing the cognitive load required to process these subtle signs.

One of the most effective ways to improve at identifying emotions accurately is to engage in regular practice. Observing people in various settings—whether it's in a workplace meeting, a casual conversation, or while watching interviews—can sharpen your skill. The more diverse the scenarios you expose yourself to, the more adept you become at picking up these universal facial indicators of emotion. Combining practice with reflection will give you insights into common patterns and anomalies in emotional expression.

Feedback is invaluable in this learning process. This could be through self-reflection, asking colleagues for their perspectives, or using technological tools designed for training in emotional intelligence. Structured feedback loops can greatly enhance your understanding and ability to identify emotions accurately. Consider keeping a journal of your observations and reflecting on them regularly to fine-tune your skills.

Another important aspect of accurately identifying emotions is to clear your own emotional biases. It's easy to project your feelings or expectations onto others, which can cloud your judgment. Being aware of your own emotional state and striving for neutrality when observing others will improve accuracy. Regular mindfulness practices can help in achieving this emotional clarity, keeping you present and more observant.

Building a strong foundation in the anatomy of facial expressions helps demystify the process. Knowing which muscles are involved in forming different expressions can make it easier to spot those rapid micro-expressions. For instance, understanding that a genuine smile involves the orbicularis oculi muscles around the eyes, not just the zygomatic major muscles lifting the mouth, makes it more apparent when a smile is genuine or forced.

Self-awareness is critical. Regularly checking in with your own emotional state can help you separate your emotions from what you observe in others. This self-regulation ensures that you respond to others based on their feelings, not a misinterpretation influenced by your own emotions. Incorporating self-awareness exercises can refine this ability over time.

To truly excel at identifying emotions, it also helps to expand your emotional vocabulary. Being able to name and categorize emotions accurately allows for more nuanced recognition and interpretation. While someone might broadly appear 'happy,' being able to discern whether they are more 'content,' 'excited,' or 'relieved' provides deeper insights and can guide a more tailored and effective response.

Educational tools like videos, interactive software, or even courses on emotional intelligence can be beneficial. These resources offer a wealth of scenarios and guided practice opportunities, enhancing your ability to spot micro-expressions. Interactive features often allow for immediate feedback, which is crucial for developing accuracy.

Group practice sessions can also be invaluable. Engaging with peers in role-playing exercises or real-time observation challenges fosters a collaborative learning environment. Sharing insights and discussing interpretations with others can broaden your understanding and improve your skill set through collective knowledge and diverse perspectives.

Empathy plays a pivotal role in identifying emotions accurately. It's not merely about recognizing what someone feels but understanding the why behind it. Developing relational empathy enhances your ability to read micro-expressions as it creates a deeper connection and understanding. Cultivating empathy allows you to anticipate and interpret these quick flashes of emotion more accurately.

Another useful strategy is to observe yourself while in different emotional states. Recording and analyzing your own facial expressions during various mood swings provides personal data for understanding micro-expressions. Self-study allows you to recognize patterns and anomalies in your own expressions, which can then be applied to observing others.

Identifying emotions accurately through the observation of micro-expressions is a skill that can revolutionize professional and personal interactions. In leadership, this skill can inform better decision-making and team management. In personal relationships, it fosters deeper connections and more meaningful communication. The capability to see beyond words to the raw emotions that people experience strengthens human bonds and enhances trust.

Remember, the journey towards mastering this skill is ongoing. Continuous learning, practicing, and reflecting will ensure your ability to identify emotions accurately evolves and sharpens over time. This journey can be as rewarding as the skill itself, offering profound insights into human nature and improving your relational dynamics on multiple levels.

Enhancing Empathy

Empathy is the cornerstone of meaningful and effective communication. Understanding another person's emotions not just broadens your social circle but also enriches it. When it comes to enhancing empathy, micro-expressions play a crucial role. They are essentially the subtle, involuntary facial movements that convey a person's genuine emotions, often before they even articulate them. By mastering the art of recognizing these micro-expressions, you can significantly improve your empathetic skills, turning abstract emotional intelligence into actionable insight.

The first step in enhancing empathy through micro-expressions is to become an observer. Real empathy involves paying attention, not just superficially, but deeply. Watch the spaces between smiles, the slight furrowing of the brow, and even the twitch of an eye. These are not just random facial movements; they are signals, giving you a window into another person's emotional state. When you start to decode these cues, you shift from simply hearing words to truly understanding feelings, making your interactions more enriched.

One of the practical ways to sharpen your empathetic skills is through mindfulness. Mindfulness isn't just a trendy buzzword; it's a valuable practice that keeps you in the present moment. When you're engaged and attentive, you're more likely to pick up on the micro-expressions that flit across someone's face. Rigorous mindfulness exercises can enhance your ability to notice even the most fleeting of expressions, which often reveal the truest emotions. With persistent practice, this can become second nature.

Imagine you're in a team meeting, and a colleague mentions a new project timeline that seems impractically tight. You notice a quick flash of fear or frustration on their face before they mask it with a smile. Recognizing that micro-expression gives you a deeper understanding of their genuine concerns, opening up opportunities for empathetic dialogue. You might say, "I sensed this timeline might be worrying you—do you want to talk about it?" This approach not only validates their feelings but also fosters a sense of trust.

Enhancing empathy through micro-expressions also involves reflecting on your own emotional responses. Self-awareness is a crucial aspect of emotional intelligence. When you understand how you react to various triggers, you can better manage your emotions and respond more empathetically to others. This reflective practice helps you build a strong foundation, making you more receptive to others' emotional cues.

Putting yourself in someone else's shoes is often easier said than done. However, practicing perspective-taking can greatly enhance your empathetic skills. This can be done through role-playing exercises where you consciously try to experience situations from someone else's viewpoint. When you combine this with the ability to read micro-expressions, your understanding of others' emotions becomes more comprehensive and nuanced, enabling you to respond with greater empathy.

Active listening goes hand-in-hand with recognizing micro-expressions. It's not just about listening to the words; it's about tuning into the underlying emotions. By focusing on what lies beneath the surface, you create a space where people feel truly heard and understood. It's an active process requiring attention and responsiveness, but the payoff is worth it as relationships become more authentic and meaningful.

Technology can also be an ally in this endeavor. Various tools and software are designed to help individuals practice and enhance their understanding of micro-expressions. These tools provide real-time feedback, helping you sharpen your skills in recognizing subtle emotional cues. While technology should not replace human interaction, it can certainly complement your learning process, making you more adept at empathy.

Incorporating feedback into your practice is essential. Whether it comes from peers, mentors, or even technology, feedback helps you understand your strengths and areas for improvement. This continuous loop of learning and refinement is crucial in mastering the art of empathy. Over time, your ability to recognize and respond to emotional cues will become more intuitive and accurate.

Empathy is not just a personal skill; it's a transformative tool in leadership. Leaders who can understand and resonate with their team's emotions are more likely to create a motivating and supportive work environment. By honing your ability to read micro-expressions, you can become a leader who inspires trust and loyalty, fostering a culture of openness and collaboration.

Enhancing empathy has a ripple effect. When you show empathy, it encourages others to do the same. This can create a more compassionate and understanding environment, whether it's in the workplace, at home, or within your community. Your ability to recognize and respond to others' emotions sets a precedent for meaningful and empathetic interactions.

One of the rewarding aspects of enhancing empathy is the improvement in personal relationships. Empathy allows you to connect on a deeper level, fostering trust and intimacy. By reading the micro-expressions of your loved ones, you can better understand their needs and emotions, leading to more meaningful and supportive relationships.

Ethical considerations cannot be ignored. As you get better at reading micro-expressions, it's important to use this skill responsibly. The goal is to enhance empathy and build better connections, not to manipulate or deceive. Always approach this knowledge with a mindset of mutual respect and understanding, prioritizing ethical interactions above all.

Empathy is a journey, not a destination. As you develop and hone your skills in recognizing micro-expressions, remember that it involves continuous learning and practice. The more you engage with people, the more you'll understand the complexities of human emotion. This ongoing commitment to growth will make your empathetic skills more refined and effective.

Ultimately, the mastery of micro-expressions to enhance empathy equips you with a powerful tool. It transforms your interactions, making them richer and more meaningful. This skill bridges gaps in understanding, fostering deeper connections and more authentic relationships. As you integrate this knowledge into your daily life, you'll find yourself becoming not just a better communicator, but a more compassionate and empathetic person.

Chapter 6:
Micro-Expressions in the Workplace

Navigating the intricate landscape of workplace dynamics can feel like walking a tightrope, but mastering micro-expressions offers a safety net that can transform your professional environment. Imagine a manager who unlocks their team's unspoken concerns through a furrowed brow or an unexpected grin; this subtle awareness can catalyze change and drive results. Enhancing leadership skills often means more than giving orders—it's about tuning into these fleeting flashes of emotion to decode underlying issues and foster a more cohesive team. When leaders and colleagues tap into micro-expressions, they bolster not just productivity, but mutual understanding and respect. Harnessing the power of these silent signals could be the key to transforming conflicts into opportunities and turning ordinary meetings into powerful connections. This chapter dives deep into how these tiny, almost imperceptible cues could revolutionize teamwork, build stronger bonds, and create a workplace where every member feels truly seen and heard.

Improving Leadership Skills

Improving leadership skills is a journey, and understanding micro-expressions can significantly enhance how leaders navigate this path. When we talk about leadership, we're not just referring to the ability to make decisions or delegate tasks. True leadership involves subtler aspects, like the ability to read and respond to the unspoken concerns of a team. This is where micro-expressions come into play, acting as potent indicators of underlying emotions that words alone may not convey.

When a leader becomes adept at recognizing micro-expressions, they gain an invaluable tool. These tiny, fleeting facial cues can reveal a lot about an individual's true feelings, even when they attempt to mask them. Imagine walking into a meeting and within seconds sensing who might be anxious, who feels confident, or who might have reservations about the discussed agenda. This insight can drive more empathetic and impactful interactions.

One of the initial steps in mastering this skill is to develop a keen eye for detail. Micro-expressions occur in less than a second, and they can be easy to miss if you're not paying attention. Leaders who cultivate a habit of observing rather than just seeing are better positioned to catch these subtle indicators. For example, a quick flash of fear or surprise might suggest someone is not fully on board with a plan. Addressing such sentiments promptly can prevent misunderstandings and foster an environment of openness.

Regular practice is another cornerstone of building this skill. Using resources like video recordings of meetings can be particularly effective. Analyzing these recordings allows leaders to pause and review moments that they might have missed in real time. This isn't just about recognizing micro-expressions but also understanding their context and accurately interpreting them. Various tools and training programs can also aid in this process, offering structured methodologies to identify and interpret these fleeting expressions.

Improving leadership skills through micro-expressions also involves enhancing one's emotional intelligence. Leaders who are emotionally intelligent are often more successful, as they can empathize with their team and make informed decisions based on emotional cues. Recognizing micro-expressions feeds directly into this, allowing leaders to read the room more effectively and adjust their approach accordingly. For instance, a brief look of contempt from a team member might signal underlying disagreements that need to be addressed.

Furthermore, understanding micro-expressions helps in conflict resolution. Leaders who can detect the smallest signs of distress or disagreement are in a better position to address issues before they escalate. Early intervention can transform potentially volatile situations into opportunities for growth and understanding. This proactive approach not only mitigates conflict but also builds a culture of trust and transparency within the organization.

Another key advantage is the ability to inspire and motivate the team. Leaders who are attuned to their team's emotional states can offer targeted support and encouragement. When a leader notices a flash of doubt or hesitation, they can offer reassurance or additional information to alleviate concerns. This tailored support fosters a sense of being understood and valued, which can significantly boost morale and productivity.

The ripple effect of improving leadership skills through the understanding of micro-expressions also extends to making more informed decisions. Leaders often need to make quick judgments based on incomplete information. In such scenarios, the ability to gauge the team's unspoken feelings can provide crucial additional data points. For example, a unanimous nod in agreement with a policy might be accompanied by fleeting looks of doubt or unease, signaling the need for further discussion or contemplation before moving forward.

Moreover, the role of authenticity in leadership cannot be understated. Leaders who show genuine concern and responsiveness to their team's unspoken concerns build stronger relationships. This authenticity is crucial for long-term success and helps prevent the disconnect that can occur when leaders are perceived as being out of touch with their team's reality.

Equally important is the impact on personal growth. Leaders who invest in understanding micro-expressions cultivate a habit of continuous learning. This constant sharpening of observation and interpretation skills is not just a professional asset but a personal one. It enhances one's ability to connect on a deeper level with others, whether in a professional or personal context.

Finally, leveraging micro-expressions for improving leadership skills is not a solitary endeavor. Mentorship and collaboration within leadership circles can accelerate this learning process. Sharing experiences, discussing different micro-expressions observed, and their interpretations can provide broader perspectives and richer insights. The value of a collective approach cannot be overstated in this regard.

In essence, the journey of improving leadership skills through understanding micro-expressions is a multifaceted one. It's about developing an eye for subtle cues, practicing regularly, enhancing emotional intelligence, resolving conflicts proactively, inspiring and motivating teams, making informed decisions, and embracing authenticity. This journey not only makes one a better leader but also enriches one's understanding of human interactions, paving the way for more genuine and effective leadership.

Enhancing Team Dynamics

The dynamics within a team are pivotal to its success, and understanding micro-expressions can dramatically enhance how team members interact and collaborate. Micro-expressions offer a window into the unspoken emotions of your colleagues - a fleeting glimpse that can reveal more than words ever could. By tuning into these subtle cues, leaders and team members alike can create a more cohesive and emotionally intelligent environment, fostering both productivity and job satisfaction.

Micro-expressions provide a critical edge in building stronger team dynamics because they help reveal underlying feelings and attitudes that are often concealed. Imagine sitting in a team meeting where a colleague's fleeting frown goes unnoticed while discussing a key project. This micro-expression could indicate disagreement or concern about the project's direction. Recognizing these subtle cues allows leaders to address issues in real-time, before they escalate into larger problems. This preemptive problem-solving can transform team culture, making it more open and effective.

Creating an environment where every team member feels understood and valued begins with the leader's ability to read and respond to micro-expressions. When team members sense that their emotions are being acknowledged, their commitment to the team's objectives grows. Leaders can use micro-expression recognition to provide more tailored feedback, support, and motivation. For instance, if a team member shows signs of anxiety through a brief lip press, a leader can offer reassurance or clarity about their role, dissolving tension and building trust.

Understanding and responding to micro-expressions also cultivates an atmosphere of empathy within the team. When leaders and colleagues are attuned to one another's emotional states, they're more likely to offer support and understanding. This kind of support is invaluable during stressful periods, such as meeting tight deadlines or navigating organizational changes. The ability to intuitively grasp a team member's emotional state builds a safety net of empathy, encouraging individuals to express themselves more openly.

Empathy goes beyond merely recognizing emotions; it involves taking action to address the underlying causes of these emotions. For example, if a team member shows a brief look of surprise during a regular meeting, it might signal something unexpected or unclear. By addressing these moments and seeking clarification, leaders can ensure that everyone is on the same page, fostering a more inclusive and transparent work environment. This not only improves team dynamics but also accelerates problem-solving and innovation.

Another essential aspect of enhancing team dynamics through micro-expressions is the ability to mediate conflicts effectively. Teams, by nature, consist of diverse individuals with varying perspectives, which inevitably leads to disagreements. However, with the skill to recognize and interpret micro-expressions, leaders can detect potential conflicts before they become overt issues. A slight narrowing of the eyes or a quick glance away can signify disapproval or discomfort. Addressing these signs early can prevent conflicts from escalating, maintaining harmony and productivity.

Moreover, team members themselves benefit from recognizing each other's micro-expressions. It encourages peer-to-peer empathy and collaboration. When individuals feel that their teammates perceive and respect their emotional states, they're more likely to share ideas and provide constructive feedback. This collective empathy creates a supportive environment, promoting risk-taking and creativity. In competitive industries, fostering such an atmosphere can be the difference between stagnation and breakthrough innovation.

Enhancing team dynamics through micro-expressions isn't just about solving problems; it's about harnessing the full potential of each team member. Recognizing moments of enthusiasm, excitement, or curiosity can also be incredibly powerful. These positive micro-expressions often signal opportunities for growth, learning, and collaboration. Leaders who are adept at spotting and encouraging these positive signals can drive their teams towards greater achievements.

One practical way to incorporate micro-expression recognition into daily team interactions is through regular check-ins and feedback sessions. During these meetings, pay attention not just to what is being said, but also how it's being said - the facial expressions accompanying the words. Are there smiles of genuine enthusiasm? Or perhaps fleeting looks of concern or doubt? By integrating these observations into your feedback process, you create a more holistic understanding of your team's morale and dynamics.

Training team members to recognize and respond to micro-expressions can be equally beneficial. Workshops and exercises focused on emotional intelligence and non-verbal communication can empower everyone in the team to become more adept observers. This collective skill-building enhances overall communication, reducing misunderstandings and fostering a culture of mutual respect and empathy.

It's also worth noting that the physical workspace itself plays a role in how well micro-expressions can be observed and interpreted. Open spaces that promote visibility and interaction can make it easier for team members to pick up on each other's cues. However, it's also essential to provide private spaces where individuals can retreat when they need to manage their emotions without an audience. Balancing these elements can create a supportive environment where micro-expressions are more readily observable and actionable.

Furthermore, technology can enhance our ability to recognize and respond to micro-expressions. Tools such as video conferencing software with high-resolution capabilities can help maintain this level of interpersonal connection, even in remote settings. Being aware of how micro-expressions translate over a screen can help teams maintain the nuanced understanding of emotions that is essential for effective communication and collaboration.

The journey to mastering the art of recognizing and responding to micro-expressions in the workplace is ongoing. It requires continuous practice, awareness, and a genuine commitment to understanding others. However, the rewards are significant - enhanced team dynamics, improved emotional intelligence, and a workplace culture that values and respects the emotional well-being of every team member. By making the effort to see beyond words and tune into the emotional undercurrents of your team, you pave the way for a more cohesive, empathetic, and ultimately more successful team.

Chapter 7:
Micro-Expressions in
Personal Relationships

Personal relationships thrive on nuanced understanding, and micro-expressions serve as a hidden language that can enrich these connections. When you discern the fleeting expressions that flash across a loved one's face, you open a gateway to deeper trust and heightened emotional resonance. Imagine catching a barely noticeable flicker of sadness during a conversation; this offers a unique opportunity to address the emotion before it magnifies, thereby preventing misunderstandings. Utilizing these subtle cues, you can also navigate and resolve conflicts more efficiently. When tension arises, recognizing the genuine hurt or concern behind words can defuse situations and foster empathy. Ultimately, the ability to decode micro-expressions transforms relationships into spaces of genuine understanding and mutual respect, making every interaction more meaningful and constructive.

Building Trust

Building trust in personal relationships is fundamentally about creating a foundation where both parties feel secure, understood, and valued. Trust isn't something that happens overnight; it requires consistent effort and mutual respect. Micro-expressions, those fleeting facial signals that can reveal true emotions, play a significant role in this intricate dance of connection.

Imagine you're having a conversation with someone close to you. You say, "I really wish you'd help more around the house," and you catch a brief flash of anger or frustration before they quickly mask it with a smile. That micro-expression tells a story that their words might not. Understanding these subtle cues can help navigate tricky emotional landscapes and pave the way for deeper trust.

One of the key elements in building trust through micro-expressions is authenticity. When we perceive that someone is genuine, we're more likely to trust them. Authenticity means our facial expressions align with our words and actions. For instance, if you're expressing gratitude but your face shows contempt, the mismatch can create doubt and weaken the bond.

Active listening is another cornerstone of building trust. It goes beyond simply hearing words; it involves picking up on those non-verbal cues that provide context and depth to the spoken language. By honing the skill to recognize micro-expressions, you demonstrate that you're not just listening but truly understanding the underlying emotions. This level of empathy can significantly boost trust.

Trust is also built through emotional attunement. This means recognizing and responding to your partner's emotions in a timely and appropriate manner. If your significant other displays a micro-expression of sadness, even if briefly, addressing it with kindness and concern can make a world of difference. Ignoring these cues can create emotional distance, while acknowledging them fosters closeness and understanding.

Moreover, transparency is vital. In relationships, we often expect honesty and openness. Micro-expressions are like emotional signposts, and recognizing them helps ensure transparency. If there's a mismatch between someone's spoken statements and their micro-expressions, it signals that something might be amiss, prompting a deeper conversation and clarifying any issues.

Consistency is another important factor. Trust grows when actions are in line with words over time. Micro-expressions are a part of this consistency. When our emotions consistently match our words, others see us as reliable and trustworthy. This reliability fosters a stable environment where trust can flourish.

Building trust doesn't mean you're always in agreement. There will be conflicts, but how you handle them makes a difference. Recognizing micro-expressions during disagreements can help keep the conversation constructive. For example, if you notice a look of fear or uncertainty, it might signal that your partner isn't feeling heard or understood, guiding you to approach the situation with more sensitivity.

In addition, vulnerability plays a significant role in trust-building. When you allow yourself to be seen as you truly are, including your faults and insecurities, it invites others to do the same. Recognizing and responding to micro-expressions of vulnerability, like fleeting looks of fear or shame, can reinforce that it's safe to be open and authentic, deepening the trust between you.

Reciprocal validation is crucial as well. Trust is a two-way street; it's about giving and receiving validation. If you notice a micro-expression of joy or pride when your partner shares an achievement and you respond with genuine affirmation, it creates a cycle of positive reinforcement. Both parties feel valued and seen, which strengthens the relationship.

Trust is often tested during stress and adversity. In such times, micro-expressions become even more vital. When life throws curveballs, being able to read and react to your partner's true feelings can help navigate challenges together. For instance, during a stressful event, observing a micro-expression of despair can prompt a supportive response, rather than escalating the situation.

Creating a safe non-judgmental space is essential for trust. Micro-expressions can inadvertently convey judgment. Even a quick eyebrow raise or a micro-frown can be interpreted as disapproval. Being aware of these and consciously managing your reactions can maintain an environment where both feel accepted and free from judgment.

Building trust through micro-expressions isn't just about the big, obvious signals. It's often the little, almost imperceptible things that matter most. These fleeting moments provide a wealth of information about the emotional undercurrents in a relationship. By tuning into these signals, you create a more profound and nuanced understanding of each other's emotional worlds, which is the bedrock of trust.

Empathy is the linchpin in all of this. When you get good at recognizing and responding to micro-expressions, you naturally become more empathetic. It becomes easier to put yourself in the other person's shoes and see things from their perspective. This enhanced empathy ensures that your responses are more attuned to their needs, making the relationship more resilient and robust.

Sometimes, building trust requires addressing and resolving past hurts. These are often indicated through micro-expressions of pain, regret, or resentment. Acknowledging these feelings, even when they're briefly shown, can initiate healing conversations. Ignoring them might let unspoken issues fester, undermining trust over time.

There's also the element of predictability. When you consistently recognize and validate the other person's emotions, it creates a predictable pattern of behavior. This predictability can be incredibly reassuring and eliminates uncertainty, which is a major barrier to trust.

Lastly, mutual growth solidifies trust. When both individuals are committed to understanding and improving their emotional intelligence, it creates a forward momentum. Recognizing and responding to micro-expressions is a skill that can be developed and refined over time, fostering continuous growth in the relationship.

In conclusion, building trust through micro-expressions is an ongoing process that requires attention, empathy, and authenticity. By becoming attuned to these subtle signals and responding appropriately, you nurture an environment where trust can thrive. This creates a solid foundation for any personal relationship, empowering both individuals to connect on a deeper, more meaningful level.

Resolving Conflicts

Micro-expressions, those fleeting facial cues, serve as an unspoken language that can speak volumes in resolving conflicts in personal relationships. When emotions run high, words alone often fail to convey the depth of one's feelings. Here, our silent language steps in, providing a roadmap to better understanding and resolution. By learning to accurately read and respond to these micro-expressions, we can significantly enhance our ability to navigate disagreements and misunderstandings.

The first step towards resolving conflicts is recognizing that conflicts are a natural part of any relationship. They arise from differences in values, beliefs, and needs. Micro-expressions give us a peek into these underlying issues by revealing emotions that might otherwise remain hidden. For instance, a brief flash of anger or sadness can signal that the disagreement runs deeper than the surface issue. By paying attention to these cues, you can address the core emotions involved, rather than getting stuck in a cycle of blame and counter-blame.

Consider a situation where a couple is arguing about financial decisions. While one partner might express their concerns verbally, their fleeting micro-expressions of fear or anxiety might go unnoticed.

Observing these subtle cues can reveal that the issue may not be about the money itself, but rather fears about security or unmet emotional needs. Acknowledging these emotions can pave the way for more empathetic communication, helping both parties feel heard and understood.

Empathy is the cornerstone of conflict resolution, and micro-expressions can function as empathy's guideposts. When you see a micro-expression of sadness or disappointment, it's an invitation to delve deeper. You might say, "I noticed you seemed really upset when we discussed this topic. Can we talk about what's really bothering you?" This approach not only validates the other person's feelings but also opens up space for genuine dialogue. It's about moving from confrontation to collaboration.

Importantly, it's not just about recognizing the other person's micro-expressions; it's also about being aware of your own. Self-awareness allows you to monitor and manage your emotional responses, ensuring that you communicate more effectively. For example, if you catch yourself exhibiting a fleeting micro-expression of disdain or frustration, take a moment to recalibrate. Understanding your non-verbal cues can help you approach the conversation with a more open and constructive mindset.

Timing is another critical factor. Recognizing micro-expressions allows for timely intervention. Catching an expression of resentment or disappointment early on in a discussion can prevent these emotions from festering. Addressing issues promptly, while the emotions are still fresh, can keep small disagreements from escalating into bigger conflicts. Think of it as a form of emotional triage, where you address the most pressing feelings first, which can often resolve the conflict more quickly and effectively.

Let's not forget the importance of context when reading micro-expressions in conflict situations. Context provides the backdrop that makes these fleeting expressions more intelligible. For example, an eye-roll may mean different things in different contexts. In one scenario, it could indicate frustration, while in another, it might be a playful gesture. Understanding the context helps in interpreting the micro-expressions accurately, thereby avoiding misjudgments that could further exacerbate the conflict.

Also, building trust is essential for resolving conflicts, and micro-expressions play an integral role in this process. Trust is predicated on feelings of safety and authenticity, elements that are often conveyed through honest non-verbal communication. When you demonstrate that you recognize and respect the other person's emotions (even the ones they may not be verbalizing), you build a foundation of trust. This trust, in turn, makes it easier to resolve conflicts because both parties feel secure enough to express their true feelings without fear of judgment or misunderstanding.

Listening is another crucial skill in resolving conflicts. Active listening goes beyond just hearing words; it involves observing the full spectrum of communication, including micro-expressions. When you listen attuned to these subtle facial cues, you capture the unspoken dimensions of the conversation. This heightened level of awareness can make your responses more attuned and aligned with the other person's emotional state. As a result, the dialogue becomes more resonant and solutions more attainable.

For leaders and professionals, mastering the art of reading micro-expressions can have substantial benefits not only in personal relationships but also in professional settings. When conflicts arise in the workplace, the ability to identify and address underlying emotions can maintain team cohesion and productivity. Imagine mediating a dispute between colleagues and being able to decode their true concerns through micro-expressions. This skill transforms you from a mere participant to an effective mediator who can navigate complex emotional landscapes.

Training yourself to recognize these micro-expressions doesn't require extraordinary innate skills; it's about practice and mindfulness. Start by observing people in low-stakes environments—like while watching a movie or during casual conversations with friends. Over time, you'll find your ability to notice and interpret these subtle cues improves, allowing you to apply them to more critical situations, such as conflict resolution in personal relationships. Gradually, what starts as a conscious effort becomes second nature, making you more adept at reading and responding to non-verbal cues effortlessly.

Conflict resolution isn't just about quelling immediate disagreements; it's about fostering long-term relational health. Micro-expressions offer valuable insights that enable us to address not just the symptoms but the root causes of conflicts. By becoming fluent in this silent language, you contribute to a more harmonious and emotionally intelligent environment, whether at home or work.

Ultimately, the goal is not to stifle conflicts—after all, disagreements can be a sign of a healthy, dynamic relationship. Rather, by utilizing the power of micro-expressions, we can approach conflicts with a toolkit designed for deeper understanding and meaningful resolution. In doing so, we transform potential points of contention into opportunities for growth, learning, and connection.

Chapter 8:
Cultural Variations and Their Impact

In our interconnected world, understanding the nuances of cultural variations in non-verbal communication can significantly enhance your ability to read micro-expressions accurately. While some facial cues are universal—smiling generally conveys happiness; frowning, displeasure—context is everything. For instance, a firm handshake might signal confidence in one culture but could be perceived as aggressive or inappropriate in another. Similarly, maintaining eye contact could be interpreted as respect in Western cultures but seen as confrontational in many Asian or African contexts. Being attuned to these differences isn't just about avoiding misunderstandings; it's about fostering deeper connections. By appreciating the subtle, culture-specific cues, you become more adept at navigating cross-cultural interactions, whether in a global workplace or diverse social setting. The beauty and challenge of mastering this skill lie in the delicate balance between recognizing universal emotional expressions and respecting the rich tapestry of cultural diversity that shapes them.

Universal vs. Culture-Specific Cues

Understanding non-verbal communication isn't just about reading a smile or a frown; it's about interpreting a complex array of signals that can vary significantly across cultures. When we dive into the realm of non-verbal cues, two main categories emerge—universal cues and culture-specific cues.

Universal cues are those signals that seem to be consistent across various cultures and contexts. For instance, a smile is generally recognized as a sign of happiness, a frown as a sign of displeasure. These cues are often rooted in our shared human biology and psychology. They tap into our fundamental emotions, which are universally understandable. Babies, for example, exhibit basic emotions like joy and anger that anyone can recognize, regardless of cultural background.

However, even these universal cues can be influenced by individual experiences and societal norms. For example, while a smile is typically associated with happiness, in some cultures, it can also be a way to mask discomfort or to avoid conflict. Therefore, even seemingly straightforward cues should be interpreted with some caution.

On the other hand, culture-specific cues are those gestures, expressions, and behaviors that have unique meanings within a particular cultural context. These are the cues that can trip you up if you're not familiar with the local customs and etiquette. A thumbs-up might mean approval in many Western cultures but could be an offensive gesture in parts of the Middle East. The "OK" hand sign is another example; while it means "okay" or "good" in many countries, it's considered rude in some South American cultures.

Decoding these culture-specific cues requires a deep understanding of the traditions, social norms, and values of the culture you're interacting with. It also demands a readiness to learn and adapt. The upside is that getting these cues right can build stronger, more authentic relationships with colleagues, friends, and clients from different backgrounds.

To navigate the complexities of culture-specific cues, one of the most effective strategies is immersion and observation. If you're relocating to a new country for work, investing time in understanding the local customs can pay off significantly. Attend social gatherings, observe how locals interact, and don't hesitate to ask questions. People generally appreciate when you make an effort to understand and respect their culture.

One striking aspect is how different cultures interpret and utilize personal space. In many Western cultures, maintaining a certain physical distance during interaction is a norm—too close, and you might be invading personal space. However, in many Latin American, Middle Eastern, and some Asian cultures, standing close to one another is a sign of trust and intimacy. Misinterpreting these cues can lead to discomfort or even conflict, so being mindful of such distinctions is essential.

Eye contact is another cue that varies widely across cultures. In the United States and many European countries, direct eye contact is considered a sign of confidence and sincerity. But in some East Asian cultures, prolonged eye contact might be seen as confrontational or disrespectful. Within Middle Eastern cultures, eye contact norms can also shift depending on gender dynamics. Understanding these subtleties can significantly impact the way your message is received.

Handshake customs also present a minefield of cultural variation. While a firm handshake is often considered a mark of strength and reliability in many Western nations, the same might be perceived as aggressive in some Asian cultures, where a gentler handshake is preferred. Moreover, the duration of the handshake and who initiates it can vary, making it even more challenging to get this simple gesture right.

Facial expressions, while largely universal in displaying emotions like happiness, sadness, and anger, can still have different intensities and acceptabilities in various cultures. For example, Japanese culture often values subtlety and restraint, so you might not see the same level of exuberance in a smile or the same intensity in a frown as you would in many Western cultures. Recognizing these cultural nuances can help you navigate social interactions more effectively.

Understanding these cues is particularly crucial in a business context. Consider the high-stakes nature of negotiations. Misreading a culture-specific cue could mean the difference between sealing a deal and losing it. Something as simple as interrupting someone might be acceptable in more fast-paced cultures but can be seen as terribly rude and dismissive in others that value turn-taking and listening.

The complexity of non-verbal communication adds layers to our understanding of it, making it a lifelong learning process. That's why adaptability and continuous learning are your best assets. The more familiar you are with different cultural cues, the more adept you become at navigating these varied social landscapes.

In conclusion, universal cues serve as the baseline in our understanding of non-verbal communication, offering a common ground across different cultures. But it's the culture-specific cues that add depth, color, and complexity to our interactions. Mastering these cues requires not only cognitive effort but also emotional intelligence and cultural sensitivity. It's this mastery that can elevate your communication skills, making you not just a better communicator but a more empathetic and understanding individual.

Human interactions are nuanced and intricate, enriched by the diversity of universal and culture-specific cues. Keen observation, respectful curiosity, and an open mind are your tools in this journey. By honing these skills, you're not just learning to decode non-verbal communication; you're stepping into the shoes of another person, understanding their world, and building bridges that cross cultural divides.

Navigating Cross-Cultural Interactions

One of the most complex and rewarding challenges in communication is navigating cross-cultural interactions. In a world that's increasingly interconnected, professionals, leaders, and individuals aiming to elevate their interpersonal skills must be mindful of cultural nuances. The landscape of cross-cultural communication is rich with opportunities and potential pitfalls alike. From boardrooms to casual conversations, understanding how cultural variations influence interaction can either create bridges or build barriers.

First off, it's imperative to realize that cultural norms heavily influence non-verbal cues. What may be considered a gesture of respect in one culture can be perceived quite differently in another. For example, direct eye contact can be seen as a sign of confidence in some Western cultures, while it might be considered disrespectful in some Asian cultures. Hence, when we're aiming to decode non-verbal cues, understanding the cultural context is not just beneficial, it's crucial.

Different cultures have distinct 'non-verbal languages.' These include gestures, facial expressions, and spatial habits. In Latin America, a warm embrace or a double cheek kiss is customary; in Japan, a bow may be more appropriate. These subtle signals convey respect, camaraderie, or even authority. Ignoring or misinterpreting them can lead to misunderstandings, even conflicts. Hence, acquiring a nuanced understanding of these cues is fundamental.

Another aspect to ponder is time orientation. Cultures vary in their perspectives on time, which affects punctuality and deadlines. In a monochronic culture like Germany, punctuality is a sign of professionalism. Contrastingly, in many polychronic cultures such as those in the Middle East, flexibility with time is expected, as relationships often take precedence over rigid schedules. Recognizing these differences can significantly enhance your ability to build rapport and manage expectations.

One might wonder, isn't there any universal aspect to non-verbal communication? Surprisingly, yes. While micro-expressions related to basic emotions like joy, sadness, anger, and fear tend to be universally recognized, their interpretation can still vary due to cultural overlays. Contextualizing these expressions within the cultural backdrop can offer more accurate insights. For instance, a smile might generally indicate friendliness, but the depth and context of the smile can vary profoundly across cultures.

The relevance of cultural awareness extends into professional realms as well. Business negotiations, for instance, can be greatly influenced by cultural etiquettes. In some cultures, a firm handshake seals the deal, while in others, a verbal agreement followed by a detailed contract might be the norm. Understanding these subtleties can position you as a more competent and empathetic negotiator. More importantly, it demonstrates respect for the other party's cultural norms, fostering mutual trust.

Empathy is another cornerstone of effective cross-cultural communication. By putting yourself in another's shoes, you not only become more attuned to their non-verbal cues but also capable of adjusting your own. This leads to more meaningful interactions. Learning a few phrases in the local language, showing interest in cultural traditions, or even simple gestures like dressing appropriately can go a long way. These actions reflect genuine interest and respect, softening any cultural barriers.

It's also necessary to be cautious of stereotypes. While cultural generalizations can provide a framework, they shouldn't be determinative. Individuals are more than the sum of their cultural backgrounds. By treating each person as a unique individual, you maintain the flexibility to adapt your non-verbal communication patterns in real-time. This adaptability is an invaluable skill in any professional or personal setting.

Let's talk about power distance for a moment. This concept refers to how power hierarchies are perceived in different cultures. In high power distance cultures like India or Mexico, showing deference to authority figures is commonplace. This could manifest as physical space, body language, or even vocal tone. Conversely, low power distance cultures such as the Netherlands emphasize equality and open communication. Understanding these dynamics allows for smoother navigation through social structures without unintentionally offending or alienating others.

Additionally, adaptability and continuous learning are key. The cultural landscape is dynamic, and what might hold true today can evolve. Hence, investing time in learning about new cultures and staying updated on global trends can be highly beneficial. Reading books, attending workshops, or simply engaging with diverse groups can enrich your cultural understanding, making you more effective in decoding non-verbal cues across different settings.

One of the most practical ways to hone your skills in navigating cross-cultural interactions is through role-playing exercises. These allow you to anticipate potential challenges and rehearse appropriate responses. By simulating real-world scenarios, you can better prepare for actual engagements. Role-playing not only boosts your confidence but also ensures that your reactions are more instinctual and culturally sensitive.

Don't underestimate the power of observation. Spend time observing interactions between individuals from different cultures. Notice how they greet each other, the physical space they maintain, and their body language during conversations. This can provide a wealth of information and help you fine-tune your own responses. Sometimes, what's left unsaid can be as impactful as what is actually spoken.

Feedback is another essential component. You can improve significantly by seeking feedback from those who are more experienced in cross-cultural interactions. Constructive criticism helps you identify areas for improvement and reinforces your strengths. Whether it's from a mentor, a colleague, or even friends from diverse backgrounds, feedback can act as a guide on your journey to becoming adept at cross-cultural communication.

Lastly, let's remember that navigating cross-cultural interactions isn't about perfection; it's about growth and improvement. Missteps are inevitable, but they also serve as learning opportunities. What's more important is your willingness to learn and adapt. By cultivating an open mind and a compassionate heart, you can navigate cross-cultural interactions with grace and effectiveness.

In sum, navigating cross-cultural interactions requires a blend of awareness, empathy, adaptability, and continuous learning. By honing these skills, you can decode non-verbal cues more accurately, enrich your professional and personal relationships, and foster a more inclusive environment. It's about creating a space where different cultural identities are respected and valued, allowing for more meaningful and successful interactions in all realms of life.

Chapter 9:
Deception Detection

In the realm of professional communication, detecting deception isn't just a useful skill; it's a necessity. Understanding deception is about recognizing inconsistencies that hint at underlying truths. Often, deceptive cues surface when verbal and non-verbal messages don't align. For example, a person might vehemently assert their honesty while their body language betrays them with subtle cues like averted eyes, crossed arms, or altered speech patterns. Key signs include micro-expressions, like fleeting facial movements contradicting spoken words, or stress-induced behaviors like fidgeting or excessive blinking. Mastering deception detection not only sharpens one's observational skills but also deepens emotional intelligence, enabling professionals to navigate complex interactions more effectively. By honing these insights, leaders and communicators can foster environments of trust, transparency, and authenticity, pivotal attributes for thriving in both personal and professional landscapes.

Recognizing Inconsistencies

Human beings are intricate mosaics of behavior, often driven by subconscious motives and desires. While most of us manage our words with some measure of control, our bodies often tell a different story. Recognizing inconsistencies between verbal and non-verbal communication is a powerful tool for detecting deception. When the body and words don't align, it's often a red flag indicating that something is askew.

Imagine you're in a meeting, and a colleague vehemently declares, "I'm very confident in this project." Their words suggest assurance, but their body language tells another tale. Perhaps their arms are crossed, a defensive posture, or they can't hold eye contact. These contradictions are critical to uncovering the truth. Inconsistencies like these are the fissures where doubt and deceit tend to reside.

Micro-expressions, the fleeting, involuntary facial expressions that reveal genuine emotions, can be your best allies in this process. These tiny signals are difficult to fake and often contradict spoken words. For example, a quick flash of fear might dart across someone's face just before they say, "I'm okay." This subtle clue suggests that their internal experience doesn't match their verbal claim.

When it comes to recognizing inconsistencies, tone of voice plays an essential role. The pitch, pace, and volume of speech can betray underlying distress or deception. A person might say they're fine, but if their voice wavers or their speech is noticeably hurried, it's worth considering that they might be hiding their true feelings or intentions.

But it's not just about catching lies. Recognizing inconsistencies can also illuminate genuine misunderstandings or unvoiced concerns, paving the way for improved communication and trust. For instance, employees who seem inexplicably hesitant or dissatisfied during meetings might reveal more about their true sentiments through their body language than their words. Leaders who can detect these non-verbal cues can address issues proactively.

Cross-referencing is an invaluable technique. Let's say a team member recounts an event but their physical expressions, vocal tone, and previous statements all jar with each other. Noting these discrepancies reveals layers of their experience that might otherwise remain hidden. By understanding these variances, leaders and professionals can navigate workplace dynamics more effectively.

Even the smallest of gestures, like a shrug or a momentary smirk, can speak volumes. A person's baseline behavior—how they normally act—is essential for identifying deviations. When someone starts acting out of character, this shift can signal that something's amiss. It's about developing a keen eye and an intuitive sense for these discrepancies.

According to various studies, including those by renowned psychologists and communication experts, the credibility of a message is often called into question by visible hesitation or confusion in the speaker's body language. The incongruence between their intended message and their physical delivery creates cognitive dissonance in the observers' minds, planting seeds of doubt about the message's authenticity.

Consider a situation where a manager needs to inspire confidence in a new strategy. If they stand tall, speak calmly, and maintain steady eye contact, their non-verbal cues support their message of confidence. If, instead, they avoid eye contact, fiddle with their hands, or exhibit erratic speech patterns, these inconsistencies undermine their credibility. Recognizing and addressing these inconsistencies can be the difference between successful leadership and ineffective management.

Drilling down deeper, a wealth of deceptive cues can be subtle yet telling. Repeating the same phrases, over-justifying actions, or providing too much unnecessary detail are often indicators that someone is trying to convince not just the listener, but also themselves of their narrative. Being keenly aware of these verbal patterns, combined with non-verbal inconsistencies, sharpens your ability to detect deception.

Emotional intelligence (EQ) is at the core of effectively recognizing these inconsistencies. Those with high EQ can intuit the complex interplay of verbal and non-verbal signals, making it easier to spot when things don't add up. Cultivating emotional intelligence isn't just about perception; it also involves empathy. By understanding where a person's incongruencies come from, you can address underlying issues directly and compassionately.

Interrogators and psychologists often leverage these principles every day, but these skills are not reserved exclusively for them. Practicing mindfulness can hone your observational skills. By staying present and observant in your interactions, you can notice subtle shifts in expression and tone that might otherwise go unnoticed.

Practical exercises can vastly improve your ability to spot inconsistencies. Role-playing scenarios where you look for discrepancies between what's being said and what's being expressed physically can be very effective. Over time, these exercises can train your mind to naturally pick up on discordances as they arise in real-life interactions.

Technology offers additional layers of support in this arena as well. Software that analyzes facial expressions, voice stress, and even body movements is becoming more advanced and accessible. These tools can provide an analytical basis to support your intuitive assessments. Imagine combining gut instinct with technology-driven insights— your ability to detect deception could reach new heights.

However, remember that context is king. Cultural differences, personal habits, and situational stress can all influence non-verbal cues. Therefore, recognizing inconsistencies isn't just about spotting red flags; it's about understanding the full tapestry of human interaction. It requires a balance of keen observation, emotional intelligence, and contextual awareness.

In every conversation, look for clusters rather than isolated signals. One inconsistency might be a fluke, but a series of discrepancies paints a larger, more intricate picture. By tuning into these patterns, you can navigate personal and professional interactions with greater clarity and insight.

In conclusion, recognizing inconsistencies is about being an active participant in your interactions rather than a passive observer. It involves a practiced eye, a mindful presence, and an empathetic heart. When words and actions don't align, the truth is often hidden in the gaps. By mastering the art of detecting these gaps, you empower yourself to communicate more effectively, build stronger relationships, and lead with greater authenticity.

Common Deceptive Cues

In the quest to better understand and identify deception, it is crucial to focus on the subtle, often overlooked cues that reveal more than spoken words. When people lie, their bodies can betray their true intentions and emotions. Learning to recognize these signals can enhance your ability to decode non-verbal cues, making you more proficient in both personal and professional interactions.

One of the most telling signs of deception is inconsistency between verbal and non-verbal messages. If someone expresses confidence verbally but displays signs of nervousness physically, such as fidgeting or avoiding eye contact, this dissonance is worth noting. Misalignment in communication suggests that the person might not be completely truthful, providing an early warning signal worth investigating further.

Micro-expressions—those fleeting, involuntary facial expressions that reveal emotions—are powerful indicators of hidden feelings. When detecting deception, a person might exhibit a micro-expression of fear, anger, or disgust while verbally discussing something benign. These micro-expressions are often masked by a more socially acceptable expression but briefly flicker across the face, offering a glimpse into the person's true emotional state.

Another common deceptive cue is overcompensation. Some people try to control their body language so tightly that they appear unnaturally stiff or overly rehearsed. For instance, an overly rigid posture or excessively controlled gestures can indicate that someone is trying too hard to manage how they are perceived. This can be a red flag, especially when the demeanor clashes with the content of their speech.

Speech patterns also matter. Lies often alter a person's usual speaking style. Irregularities such as longer pauses, stammering, or excessive hesitations can signal deception. A person might also add unnecessary details or ramble as a way to divert attention from the lie. Paying close attention to these shifts can alert you to possible dishonesty.

Then there's the matter of eye contact. Contrary to popular belief, deceptive individuals might actually maintain eye contact to appear more sincere. The key is to observe the nature of the eye contact: Is it intense to the point of being uncomfortable? Is there a lack of normal blinking? Conversely, a sudden drop in eye contact, especially during critical moments of conversation, can be equally telling.

Hand movements and gestures also provide useful information. For example, hiding hands in pockets, crossing arms, or constantly touching the face can point towards discomfort and anxiety, often seen in deceptive behavior. These small, seemingly insignificant actions can speak volumes about the unspoken tensions a person may be experiencing.

Moreover, watch out for discrepancies in facial expressions and tone of voice. If someone's tone doesn't match their facial expression—for example, they're smiling but sound tense—it's a cue that something might be off. Inconsistencies here can be subtle but are telling when they appear.

Another notable cue involves the mechanics of the head. Deceivers might exhibit a more pronounced head movement delay. This means that their head may move slightly after their words, indicating that they're buying time to fabricate their story. Additionally, rapid or continuous nodding when giving a response can imply an effort to convince both themselves and the listener of a falsehood.

Look for self-soothing behaviors, which often manifest when someone is under stress or attempting deception. These include rubbing the neck, playing with jewelry, or adjusting clothing. Such actions indicate a higher level of discomfort, hinting at potential dishonesty.

Micro-expressions, precisely because they are so short-lived, require a keen eye to detect. This adds another layer of complexity, but once mastered, they become incredibly revealing. For example, a micro-expression of contempt, marked by a slight lip curl, can indicate disdain or an attempt to dismiss the truth. Recognizing these fleeting moments equips you with invaluable information.

Body orientation is another deceptive cue. People who are lying tend to turn their bodies away from their interlocutor, a subconscious effort to create distance and protect themselves from getting caught. Conversely, someone who is being honest is more likely to squarely face the person they're conversing with.

Watch for duplicity in emotions showcased in body language. Deceptive individuals might express happiness with their mouth but sadness in their eyes. This duality can be subtle and easily missed unless you're paying close attention. It often indicates that while a person is outwardly showing one emotion, internally they are experiencing a completely different one.

You might also notice changes in breathing patterns. When someone lies, their autonomic nervous system reacts, often leading to quicker, shallower breaths. This physiological response can be subtle but is a reliable indicator of increased stress or anxiety, often accompanying deception.

Physical barriers are another cue. Someone engaged in deceptive behavior might place objects like phones, cups, or books between themselves and the person they're speaking to. This physical separation can be a subconscious attempt to create a buffer zone, providing a sense of security.

Posture dynamics can be revealing too. While confident, truthful individuals tend to display open and relaxed postures, deceivers might exhibit closed postures, such as crossing arms or legs. It's as if their bodies are reflecting the guardedness of their words.

Finally, let's not overlook the significance of vocal pitch. Lies can cause slight increases in the pitch of a person's voice. These vocal anomalies occur because of tension and nervousness, making it another auditory cue to consider when evaluating honesty.

Developing the skill to identify common deceptive cues takes time and practice. But by becoming more attuned to these subtle signals, you empower yourself with a deeper understanding of human behavior. This not only enhances your ability to detect deception but also enriches your overall communication skills, fostering more genuine connections in all areas of your life.

Chapter 10:
Non-Verbal Communication
in Virtual Spaces

In today's rapidly evolving digital age, mastering non-verbal communication in virtual spaces has become an essential skill that can significantly elevate both professional and personal interactions. Imagine navigating a video call where the subtlety of a nod helps seal a deal or a carefully timed smile hides miles of distance, connecting you instantly to your audience. With the increasing reliance on digital communication platforms, our ability to decipher and convey non-verbal cues such as facial expressions, body language, and even eye contact has never been more critical. Paying attention to these subtleties allows us to cultivate empathy, foster stronger relationships, and ensure clarity in our exchanges, despite the physical barriers that technology imposes. As we dissect the nuances of digital interaction, remember that the screen isn't just a barrier; it's a new kind of conduit, one that, when navigated skillfully, can transform the way we connect and communicate. Let's delve into the transformative power of non-verbal signals in our virtual world, ensuring that our digital presence is as impactful as our physical one.

Adapting to Digital Interactions

We live in an era where digital interactions are becoming the norm, significantly impacting how we interpret non-verbal cues. It's a brave new world of communication where facial expressions, body language, and even pauses take on new meanings. Unlike face-to-face encounters, virtual meetings come with their own set of challenges and opportunities. Adapting our non-verbal communication to these new mediums is not just beneficial—it's essential.

One of the first aspects to consider when communicating in virtual spaces is the camera. Unlike in-person meetings, where your entire body language and posture play a role, the camera typically focuses only on your face and upper torso. This limitation means facial expressions and subtle hand gestures become even more critical. A simple nod, a genuine smile, or even a raised eyebrow can convey essential emotional cues. However, one must also be mindful of the camera angle and lighting, as these can drastically affect your ability to convey expressions accurately.

No doubt, the nuances of vocal tonality cannot be overlooked when navigating virtual interactions. In a digital setting, our voice often takes on a more significant role in conveying emotions, attitudes, and even doubts. Using varied tones in speech helps to add layers of meaning to your words. Therefore, practicing vocal modulation can make a substantial difference in how your message is received. Imagine delivering praise with a monotonous voice; it likely wouldn't come across as sincere. Thus, mindful control over voice tone, speed, and pauses can enhance comprehension and connection.

But, let's take a step further and talk about eye contact. In face-to-face conversations, maintaining eye contact is crucial for building trust and showing attentiveness. In virtual settings, this becomes a challenge due to the natural tendency to look at the screen and not directly into the camera. However, making a conscious effort to occasionally look into the camera can simulate the effect of eye contact, making the interaction feel more personal and engaging. This practice, though minor, can have a profound effect on the quality of digital communication.

- Elevate your camera to eye level to create a more natural appearance.

- Ensure your background is clean and professional, free of distractions.

- Make an effort to engage with visual cues from your interlocutors observed on your screen.

Another crucial element is the realm of gestures. In physical meetings, your hand movements, head nods, or even the way you hold a pen can be powerful communicative tools. In virtual settings, these again need adjustments. With limited screen space, larger, slower gestures can help ensure that your movements are noticed. Quick or subtle movements may go unseen and thus unappreciated. Practicing these enhanced gestures can help make your non-verbal communication more effective in the digital world.

Let's also address the concept of "digital presence." This term refers to how one projects oneself in a virtual environment. It's more than just appearing on the screen; it's about exuding engagement, energy, and professionalism. Simple strategies like leaning slightly forward show interest, while sitting back can sometimes convey relaxation or disengagement. Adapting your physical stance to reflect your level of participation can make you seem more invested in the conversation.

Moving away from individual gestures and expressions, the environment in which you conduct your digital interactions also speaks volumes. Your surrounding layout, the quality of your equipment, and even your attire contribute to the perception others will have of you. A cluttered background could distract from the message you're trying to convey, while poor audio quality might cause frustration. The goal is to create an environment that's conducive to effective communication. This doesn't mean having an elaborate setup, but simple tweaks like good lighting, a clear background, and a reliable microphone can elevate the overall interaction.

Interestingly, digital interactions have highlighted the importance of pauses and silence in conversation. In face-to-face meetings, silences are often filled by visual cues or background activities. However, in virtual spaces, these silences are more pronounced and can sometimes feel awkward. Learning to embrace and effectively use these pauses is critical. Rather than rushing to fill the silence, allowing a moment for reflection can enhance the depth of the conversation. It's also a signal of active listening and can be an effective tool to show thoughtfulness and consideration.

Moreover, virtual interactions often come with time lags and technical glitches. Unlike face-to-face conversations where feedback is instant, virtual meetings may have delays that can disrupt the flow of communication. Being patient and adopting a slightly slower pace of speaking can mitigate misunderstandings. Additionally, nodding or using the chat feature to show acknowledgment can help bridge these gaps, ensuring the conversation remains fluid and productive.

We should also consider the emotional impact of these interactions. Virtual meetings can sometimes feel impersonal and detached, leading to a sense of alienation. However, making a conscious effort to express empathy and warmth can counteract this effect. Sharing personal anecdotes or acknowledging difficulties can humanize the digital interaction, making it more relatable and less clinical.

As we navigate this digital age, it's imperative to understand that the old rules don't entirely apply but must be adapted creatively. Each virtual platform, whether it be Zoom, Microsoft Teams, or Google Meet, has its own set of features and limitations. Becoming familiar with these can give you an edge in effectively conveying your message. Knowing when to use screen sharing, how to engage breakout rooms, and even utilizing emojis can add a layer of richness to your communication. By embracing these tools, you can significantly enhance your non-verbal communication.

In essence, adaptability is the cornerstone of mastering non-verbal communication in virtual spaces. We're beings of adaptation and ingenuity, and with a little effort, we can transform digital interactions into meaningful exchanges. Just as face-to-face communication requires practice and skill, so does virtual communication. The more we practice, the better we become at interpreting and conveying non-verbal cues digitally. And remember, the goal isn't perfection but continuous improvement. Embrace the opportunities these new mediums present and let your digital presence speak volumes.

Video Call Etiquette

Video calls have become an integral part of professional and personal communication. Understanding the intricacies of video call etiquette goes beyond just what you say; it's about how you present yourself. Let's dive into some of the key elements that will help you harness non-verbal communication effectively.

First, let's address the importance of your *environment*. A cluttered background can be distracting. An organized, tidy space conveys professionalism and respect for the person on the other side of the screen. A simple, plain backdrop works wonders. Remove any unnecessary items that may cause distractions. Investing in good lighting is key. Natural light is ideal, but if it's not an option, make sure your face is well-lit to avoid looking like a silhouette.

Your posture speaks volumes. Slouching can suggest a lack of interest or professionalism, while sitting up straight conveys confidence and attentiveness. Ensure your camera is at eye level. This setup not only avoids unflattering angles but also mimics face-to-face interactions more closely, fostering better engagement.

Eye contact remains crucial even in a virtual space. It's tricky because you might feel inclined to look at the other person's face on the screen, but try to focus on the camera instead. This creates the illusion of direct eye contact, which is vital for establishing connection and trust. If maintaining eye contact feels unnatural, practice by placing a small sticky note next to your webcam to remind you where to look.

Let's not overlook the role of facial expressions. Subtle nods, smiles, and other gestures can enhance conversation flow and show active engagement. However, exaggerated expressions can come off as insincere or distracting due to the proximity of the camera. Balance is key.

Hand gestures can supplement your conversation effectively. Keep them within the frame and use them sparingly to emphasize points. Overuse can become distracting and may lead to misinterpretation. Consider cultural differences as well; some gestures might be deemed inappropriate in certain cultures.

Avoid multitasking. Focusing solely on the conversation ensures you don't miss subtle cues. Glancing at your phone, checking emails, or other tasks can be quite noticeable on camera and show a lack of respect for the other participants. Close unnecessary tabs or applications that might tempt you away from the conversation at hand.

Micro-interruptions such as delays in sound or video lagging can disrupt the flow of conversation. To minimize these, ensure you have a strong internet connection and ask participants to mute themselves when not speaking. This reduces background noise and makes the conversation smoother.

Now, let's touch on the mute and unmute functionality. Mastering the art of muting when you're not speaking can prevent accidental interruptions or background noises from derailing the meeting. However, remember to unmute yourself when you need to speak owing to technical mishaps that can easily occur. Always have a quick test before the call begins to ensure everything is functioning correctly.

It's also essential to be mindful of the time. Start and end the meeting as scheduled. Respecting time boundaries shows professionalism and consideration for everyone's schedules. If a discussion needs more time, politely suggest a follow-up meeting rather than keeping participants longer than expected.

Taking turns to speak is even more pivotal in a virtual setting. Use visual or verbal cues to indicate when you've finished your point, allowing others to respond without talking over each other. A simple, "That's my thought, over to you," can provide clarity and flow.

Integration of screen sharing tools and virtual backgrounds needs a delicate approach. While screen sharing can be a fantastic way to present ideas, overloading your presentation with too many transitions or effects can be distracting. Virtual backgrounds should be used sparingly, and only if they don't distract or detract from the conversation. A poorly chosen background can overshadow your message.

Technical difficulties are inevitable. Handling them calmly and efficiently reflects your adaptability and problem-solving skills. Keep a composed demeanor and use humor gently to ease any tension that might arise due to these issues. A calm leader navigates challenges gracefully.

It's also worth considering non-verbal audio cues, such as your tone of voice. Maintaining a calm, clear, and expressive tone can prevent miscommunication and ensure your points are understood.

Avoid speaking too fast; pause between sentences to give the audience time to process what you're saying.

Lastly, reflect on your attire. Dress the part just as you would in a physical meeting. While it might be tempting to wear casual attire at home, opting for professional clothing reflects your commitment to the meeting and sets the right tone.

By observing these nuances in video call etiquette, you'll not only enhance your communication effectiveness but also build greater rapport and trust within your virtual interactions. Embrace these practices to navigate the complexities of non-verbal cues in the digital realm successfully.

Chapter 11:
Combining Verbal and
Non-Verbal Cues

There's an undeniable magic that happens when verbal and non-verbal cues align perfectly; it's like a symphony reaching its crescendo. The words you choose need to harmonize with your body language for communication to be truly effective. Imagine telling someone you're confident while your eyes dart around the room—those mixed signals muddle your message. Combining both sets of cues creates a tapestry that makes your intentions unmistakable and your stories compelling. In leadership roles, synchrony between words and gestures can inspire your team, fostering an environment of trust and innovation. Recognizing this synergy allows you to captivate an audience, whether you're giving a keynote speech or resolving a conflict. So, as you navigate through interpersonal interactions, strive for congruence; it's a master key to unlocking deeper connections and more impactful communication.

The Synergy of Communication

When we communicate, we often think of the words we use as the primary vehicle for our messages. Yet, just as important, if not more so, are the non-verbal cues that accompany our speech. The synergy between verbal and non-verbal communication creates a complete package that can significantly enhance our ability to convey a message effectively. When these elements align, they amplify the impact, ensuring our intentions are clear and our relationships more profound.

Consider a moment when you were listening to a speaker whose gestures, facial expressions, and tone all resonated with the message. That experience likely left a lasting impression on you. This happens because non-verbal cues account for a significant portion of how we interpret messages. Research has shown that up to 93% of communication effectiveness is determined by non-verbal behavioral cues. Hence, ignoring this aspect is like trying to convey a story with half the words missing.

One of the foremost ways verbal and non-verbal cues work together is through congruence. When what you say matches how you say it, your message becomes more convincing and trustworthy. For instance, consider the difference between someone saying "I'm fine" with a smile versus with a scowl. The words are the same, but the accompanying non-verbal cues paint two very different pictures. Inconsistencies between verbal statements and non-verbal signals can breed distrust, confusion, and miscommunication.

Let's take a deeper dive into the specific non-verbal cues that can enhance verbal communication. Facial expressions, postures, gestures, and eye contact are foundational elements. A nod during a conversation, for instance, can signal agreement and attentiveness, encouraging the speaker. Similarly, maintaining eye contact can convey confidence and sincerity. Each of these signals, when used appropriately, can prompt a richer, more engaging dialogue.

Imagine you're leading a team meeting. You're not just distributing tasks but motivating and inspiring your team. Your words outline the objectives, but your body language and facial expressions convey your enthusiasm and commitment. Open and expansive gestures can make you appear more authoritative and in control. A calm, steady tone can reassure your team, instilling confidence that you're well-prepared and reliable. The combination of these elements creates a holistic message that mere words alone wouldn't be capable of delivering.

Let's not overlook the role of silence in communication. Strategic pauses can be incredibly powerful. They give the listener time to process information and anticipate what comes next. This non-verbal cue can turn a simple presentation into a compelling narrative. The spaces between our words can communicate volumes, adding depth to our message and ensuring our audience remains engaged.

However, it's not just about using non-verbal cues to complement what you're saying; it's also about reading these cues in others. Being able to decode the non-verbal signals of those you're communicating with can provide invaluable insights. Notice a colleague's crossed arms? This might indicate discomfort or resistance. An elevated tone of voice paired with rapid speech could suggest anxiety or urgency. Picking up on these cues allows you to adjust your communication strategy dynamically, fostering a more responsive and empathetic interaction.

Furthermore, understanding the cultural nuances of non-verbal communication can significantly enhance your effectiveness in diverse settings. Non-verbal cues can vary significantly across cultures. A gesture that's positive in one culture could be offensive in another. The key is awareness and adaptability. In multicultural teams or international negotiations, recognizing these differences and appropriately adjusting your non-verbal communication can bridge divides and foster mutual understanding.

For professionals and leaders, mastering this interplay between verbal and non-verbal communication isn't just beneficial—it's essential. Effective communication is a cornerstone of good leadership. It allows you to build trust, articulate vision, navigate conflicts, and inspire teams. In negotiations, it can be the difference between closing a deal and watching it slip through your fingers. Whether you're in a boardroom, virtual meeting, or one-on-one conversation, the synergy of communication paves the way for success.

The digital age has brought new challenges and opportunities in this realm. While face-to-face interactions allow for the full spectrum of non-verbal cues, virtual communication requires us to be more conscious and deliberate. On a video call, for instance, maintaining eye contact can increase engagement, even though it requires looking at the camera rather than the screen. Likewise, gestures that are effective in person might need to be more pronounced to convey the same impact online. Understanding and adapting to these nuances ensures that you're still able to harness the power of non-verbal cues, even through a digital medium.

Train yourself to be more attuned to both your non-verbal cues and those of others. Practice in front of a mirror, record yourself, or seek feedback from trusted colleagues. Over time, this heightened awareness will become second nature, allowing you to communicate more effectively without needing to consciously think about every gesture or facial expression.

Ultimately, the synergy of communication is about alignment—ensuring that your words and your non-verbal cues tell the same story. This alignment fosters genuine connection, builds trust, and enhances clarity. In a world driven by relationships and interactions, mastering this balance can set you apart, paving the path to personal and professional success. Recognize the power you wield in your gestures, expressions, and tone. Combine them skillfully with your words, and you'll find yourself a more compelling, effective communicator.

Effective Storytelling

Imagine you're in a meeting where the speaker begins with, "Let me tell you a story." Instantly, the room becomes more attentive, the audience sits up a little straighter, and ears perk up. Why? Because storytelling is one of the oldest and most powerful forms of communication. By combining verbal and non-verbal cues, you can elevate the art of storytelling into an unforgettable experience for your audience.

Effective storytelling isn't just about the words you use. It's about syncing your body language with your narrative to create an immersive experience. Think of it as a dance between verbal and non-verbal elements. Each step, gesture, and facial expression should complement the rhythm of your words, adding layers of meaning and emotion.

A compelling story often starts with a strong hook. As you deliver that hook, your body language should emphasize its importance. Perhaps you lean in slightly, lowering your voice to draw people in, or widen your eyes to convey surprise. These non-verbal cues make your audience feel the tension or excitement you're trying to narrate.

Have you ever noticed how great storytellers use their hands? Hand gestures can illustrate points, depict scenes, and even embody characters. Imagine describing a tall tree; a simple upward movement of your hand can make your audience visualize its height. When these gestures align seamlessly with your spoken words, it creates a more vivid and engaging mental picture.

Let's not forget the power of facial expressions. Your face is a canvas of emotion. A genuine smile can make your audience feel warmth and openness, while a furrowed brow can convey concern or perplexity. The micro-expressions, those fleeting facial cues, often reveal the underlying emotions in your narrative, making your storytelling more authentic and relatable.

Eye contact is another critical element in effective storytelling. Engaging with your audience through direct eye contact can build trust and keep them focused. When narrating key parts of your story, maintain eye contact to underline their significance. Shifting your gaze can also guide your audience through different parts of your tale, creating dynamic engagement.

Your tone of voice is like a musical instrument in storytelling. Varying your pitch, volume, and pace can have a profound impact. A soft, slow voice can convey sorrow or suspense, while a loud, fast-paced tone can signify excitement or urgency. Using silence effectively can also be powerful, allowing your audience a moment to absorb and reflect on an important point.

Physical movements and posture can also enhance your storytelling. Moving across the stage or leaning against a podium can create a narrative journey, leading your audience through different phases of your story. A confident stance can instill authority and credibility, whereas a more relaxed posture can make you appear approachable and relatable.

Combining these verbal and non-verbal elements requires practice and awareness. Start by reflecting on past experiences where you communicated effectively. What were you doing with your hands, face, and body when you were deeply engaged in telling a story? Recreate those moments and build upon them.

Practicing in front of a mirror can be an invaluable exercise. Observe how your non-verbal cues align with your spoken words. You can even record yourself to identify areas for improvement. Pay attention to any inconsistencies between your verbal message and your body language and adjust accordingly.

Storytelling also benefits significantly from feedback. Share your story with friends or colleagues and ask them to focus on both your verbal and non-verbal communication. Did they feel a disconnect at any point? Were there moments where your body language significantly enhanced the story? Use this constructive feedback to refine your technique.

Remember, the goal isn't just to tell a story but to make your audience feel it. Emotional connection is the hallmark of effective storytelling. When your verbal narrative and non-verbal cues are aligned, the impact is profound. Your audience will not only understand your story but will feel as if they are a part of it.

Stories have the power to motivate, inspire, and bring about change. In a corporate setting, a story well-told can be the difference between a missed opportunity and a closed deal. In leadership, a compelling narrative can rally teams, foster trust, and drive collective action.

So, how can you ensure that your storytelling leaves a lasting impression? One technique is to use personal anecdotes. When sharing your own experiences, your authenticity shines through. Non-verbal cues such as genuine smiles, authentic gestures, and sincere eye contact make your story resonate more deeply.

Moreover, adapting your story to your audience is crucial. Understand their needs, interests, and cultural backgrounds. Tailoring your verbal and non-verbal cues to fit the context of your audience makes your storytelling more effective and inclusive. It's not merely about speaking but about connecting.

In today's virtual world, effective storytelling has additional layers of complexity. While physical presence might be limited, techniques such as exaggerated facial expressions and hand gestures can compensate for the lack of in-person interaction. Ensure your webcam is positioned to capture your gestures and that you maintain eye contact with the camera to engage your virtual audience.

Storytelling prepares you for diverse communication challenges in personal and professional life. It's a skill that sharpens your ability to read and project non-verbal cues effectively. It also heightens your awareness of cultural variations, equipping you to navigate cross-cultural interactions with finesse.

In essence, effective storytelling is an amalgamation of art and science. It requires the precision of understanding micro-expressions and the creativity of crafting a compelling narrative. It's about finding your unique voice while mastering the non-verbal cues that make your story come alive.

In conclusion, remember that every word, gesture, and expression has a role to play in storytelling. Strive for harmony between your verbal and non-verbal communication to create an impactful, memorable narrative. With practice, self-awareness, and the willingness to refine your skills, you can become a master storyteller. Your ability to weave together verbal and non-verbal elements will captivate your audience, making your stories not just heard, but deeply felt.

Chapter 12:
Training Yourself to Master
Micro-Expressions

Training yourself to master micro-expressions is a journey combining dedication, keen observation, and regular practice. Start by dedicating a few minutes daily to study your own facial expressions in the mirror, focusing on subtle changes. Consider leveraging technology, such as apps designed to enhance your ability to recognize fleeting emotions. Daily drills like these will build your muscle memory and sharpen your observational skills. Feedback from trusted colleagues or friends can be invaluable, offering fresh perspectives and identifying blind spots you might overlook yourself. Over time, you'll find that your ability to decode and respond to micro-expressions becomes second nature, opening doors to deeper empathy and more effective communication in both your professional and personal life. This mastery serves not only as a tool for understanding others but also as a powerful means of conveying authenticity and building strong, lasting connections. So, keep practicing and embrace the power of subtlety in every interaction.

Daily Practices

Integrating the recognition and understanding of micro-expressions into daily routines doesn't just sharpen your skills—it transforms the way you interact with the world. It's like learning a new language, one that's both mesmerizing and incredibly useful. Setting aside some time each day to practice this skill will make a significant difference in your ability to decode subtle facial cues, thereby enhancing your interpersonal communication and leadership abilities.

One simple yet highly effective practice is to engage in brief observation sessions. Dedicate five to ten minutes a day to watching videos of interviews, speeches, or even your favorite TV dramas. What you're aiming for is the capture of fleeting micro-expressions that appear during moments of emotional intensity. Pay attention to the slight flickers of the eyes, mouth, or forehead—these are often where micro-expressions reveal themselves most vividly.

It's essential to approach these daily sessions with a curious and exploratory mindset. You're not just seeing but observing, analyzing, and internalizing these subtle cues. This focused observation helps create neural pathways that make recognizing these expressions almost second nature over time. And it doesn't always have to be formal settings or planned out exercises; even paying closer attention during everyday interactions can be incredibly instructional.

Think of your social interactions as training grounds. When you're speaking with a colleague, friend, or family member, make an effort to notice their facial expressions. Are they mirroring what they're saying? Do certain topics cause fleeting signs of discomfort or joy? Over time, this conscious effort shifts into subconscious competence. You'll not only become more adept at spotting micro-expressions but also at understanding the emotions behind them.

A great daily habit to adopt is keeping an emotion journal. This isn't just a diary where you jot down what you felt during the day, but a detailed account of what you observed in others. Note the context, the micro-expressions you recognized, and how those expressions correlated with verbal communication. Reflect on how this understanding affected your response to the situation. This exercise significantly aids in reinforcing what you've learned, turning theory into practiced skill.

Incorporating role-playing exercises with a partner can also be extremely beneficial. Try to act out various scenarios where one of you exhibits a specific micro-expression in response to a particular situation. The other person should attempt to identify the emotion linked to the micro-expression. This not only makes the practice more engaging but also offers immediate feedback, which is invaluable for honing your skills.

Sometimes, technology can be your best ally. Various software programs and mobile apps are designed to help you practice identifying micro-expressions. These tools often provide an array of curated video clips and images that you can replay and analyze, catering to different skill levels. Incorporating at least 10-15 minutes of practice with these tools into your daily routine can accelerate your learning curve significantly.

Let's not forget the importance of self-awareness in this journey. Spend a few moments every day in front of a mirror, consciously mimicking different micro-expressions. By experiencing what each expression feels like on your own face, you'll develop a keener sense of empathy and recognition. This personal exploration allows you to better understand how these subtle movements convey various emotions.

In conversations, aim for an interplay of active listening and careful observation. The more you can balance listening with eye contact, the more micro-expressions you'll catch. After an interaction, take a moment to mentally review the conversation and what non-verbal cues you picked up on. Did someone's micro-expression contradict their words? Did it add another layer of meaning to what they were saying? These reviews help you refine your observational skills.

Practicing mindfulness and emotional regulation techniques is equally crucial. Being present and emotionally balanced enables you to read others more accurately. Stress and distraction can cloud your ability to pick up on subtle cues. Techniques such as deep breathing, meditation, or even a few minutes of quiet reflection can sharpen your focus, making you more adept at recognizing micro-expressions.

Lastly, continually expose yourself to diverse social environments. The more varied your interactions, the more complex and nuanced your understanding of micro-expressions will become. Attend networking events, community gatherings, or any environment where you can observe a range of emotional expressions. Each new interaction provides rich material for practice and learning.

In summary, the pathway to mastering micro-expressions is paved with consistent, daily practices that gradually weave this skill into the fabric of your everyday life. By dedicating even a small portion of your day to focused observation, role-playing, self-awareness exercises, and leveraging technology, you empower yourself to not just communicate but to connect more deeply and authentically with those around you.

Leveraging Feedback

Mastering micro-expressions is not solely about self-study and repetitive practice; it's also deeply intertwined with the act of leveraging feedback. Feedback serves as a reflective mirror, showing us the nuances and areas we might overlook in our journey to becoming adept at reading these fleeting emotional signals. The integration of feedback into your practice routine can fast-track your progress, making the learning process significantly more efficient and effective.

One of the key aspects of leveraging feedback is to be open and receptive to it. Feedback, by its very nature, can sometimes be uncomfortable or challenging, but it provides critical insights into both your strengths and areas requiring improvement. When you embrace feedback, you transform it into a tool for growth, honing your skills with precision.

Imagine practicing in front of a mirror or recording your observation exercises. While these methods can offer self-reflection, they can't replicate the multifaceted nature of interactive feedback. Engaging with a mentor, coach, or even a colleague can provide dynamic insights you might miss on your own. It's in these interactions that real-time, nuanced feedback can make a world of difference.

One approach is to seek out a diverse group of individuals who can offer different perspectives. Each person will have their own sensitivity to micro-expressions and their interpretations may vary slightly. This broadens your understanding and can help you become more adaptable in reading these cues across different individuals and contexts.

Feedback doesn't always need to come from people who are experts in micro-expressions. Sometimes, the best insights come from those who regularly interact with you in various settings. Their feedback can help you understand how your interpretation of micro-expressions translates in real-world scenarios and how it affects your communication efficiency.

Actively ask for feedback after meetings, presentations, or any interaction where you've consciously tried to observe micro-expressions. Simply asking, "Did you notice any non-verbal cues that stood out to you during our conversation?" can open a discussion that provides valuable feedback. Listen without defensiveness, and consider how you can integrate this feedback into your next interaction.

Take a structured approach to gathering feedback. Create a simple log to keep track of the feedback received, noting specific points about your micro-expression reading skills. This log can include the context of the interaction, the feedback given, and your reflections. Over time, this can become an invaluable repository of your progress and areas of focus.

Furthermore, leveraging technology can amplify your ability to capture and analyze feedback. Record video calls and review them to see if your interpretation matches the feedback you receive. This practice allows you to see both your immediate reactions and the broader context, providing a more comprehensive understanding. There are also software tools designed to analyze facial expressions and provide objective feedback, helping you fine-tune your skills.

Workshops and seminars offer another excellent platform for feedback. These settings are usually designed to provide ample opportunities for practice and feedback in a controlled environment. Participating in such events exposes you to varied scenarios and diverse feedback, enriching your learning experience.

Incorporating feedback isn't just a practical step; it's a mindset shift. It involves viewing every interaction as an opportunity for growth and improvement. This mindset fosters resilience and a continuous learning attitude, crucial for mastering the subtle art of reading micro-expressions. When receiving feedback, it's important to focus on the actionable insights rather than the delivery. Look for the core message and decide how best you can apply it to enhance your abilities.

An often-overlooked aspect of leveraging feedback is the follow-up. After receiving feedback and making adjustments, revisit those who provided insights initially. Show them the improvements you've made based on their suggestions. This not only validates their input but also reinforces your commitment to growth. Over time, this can create a supportive loop of continuous improvement.

Balancing self-assessment with external feedback is a delicate but necessary dance. While self-assessment promotes introspective growth, external feedback grounds you in the real-world efficacy of your skills. This balance ensures that you remain objective and don't develop blind spots in your interpretation of micro-expressions.

Continuous improvement is rooted in the consistency of feedback cycles. Establishing regular intervals for feedback collection ensures that you are always progressing and not slipping back into old habits. Whether it's a monthly check-in with a coach or a quarterly workshop, consistency is key.

In your professional journey, especially as leaders, the ability to read and respond to micro-expressions can significantly enhance your interpersonal skills. This, in turn, can improve team dynamics, strengthen workplace trust, and boost overall organizational health. Leveraging feedback from peers and mentors can help you understand how your improved skills impact those around you, fostering a more emotionally intelligent environment.

On a personal level, this practice extends to building more empathetic and deeper relationships. By understanding the micro-expressions of those closest to you, you can communicate more effectively, resolve conflicts quicker, and create more trust-filled connections. Feedback from loved ones about how accurately you understand their non-verbal cues can be a powerful tool for nurturing these relationships.

Finally, nurturing a growth-oriented mindset, where feedback is seen as a catalyst for improvement rather than criticism, will not only help you master micro-expressions faster but also spill over into other areas of personal and professional development. Embrace feedback as a core component of your learning process, and watch as it transforms not just your ability to read micro-expressions, but your overall effectiveness as a communicator.

Conclusion

As we draw the curtains on this exploration of non-verbal communication, it's crucial to reflect on the journey we undertook together. From delving deep into the intricate science behind micro-expressions to recognizing their profound role in emotional intelligence, we've covered significant ground. The sheer complexity and richness of human communication often lie in what is unspoken, making our journey into micro-expressions not just fascinating, but also essential for anyone aspiring to be a better leader, partner, or communicator.

The importance of non-verbal cues cannot be overstated. They are the undercurrents that shape our interactions, often speaking louder than words themselves. For professionals, being adept at reading these cues can differentiate between a successful negotiation and a missed opportunity. Leaders who master the art of decoding micro-expressions can foster more profound connections with their teams, driving higher engagement and productivity. In personal relationships, understanding these subtleties can build trust, resolve conflicts, and deepen bonds.

The practice of recognizing and interpreting micro-expressions is akin to learning a new language. It requires dedication, practice, and mindfulness. But the rewards, as we've seen, are immense. Being aware of the subtle cues people express can lead to more empathetic and effective communication. It empowers us to respond not just to what is being said, but also to the deeper emotional context behind it.

One of the standout points in our journey has been understanding that micro-expressions are universal. Regardless of cultural backgrounds, these brief flashes of emotion reveal our true feelings. However, navigating these cues in a multicultural context requires a nuanced approach. By appreciating cultural variations, we enhance our capability to communicate respectfully and effectively across different cultural landscapes.

Moreover, the evolution of our communication practices into the digital age brings about new challenges and opportunities. Virtual interactions strip away many traditional non-verbal cues, but they also offer unique ones. Video call etiquette and digital body language are realms we must master to maintain the efficacy of our interactions in this digital era.

The synthesis of verbal and non-verbal communication underscores the synergistic power of combining these elements. Effective storytelling, for instance, hinges on this synergy. Our words form the story's skeleton, while our non-verbal cues breathe life into it, making it engaging and memorable.

Ultimately, honing the skill to read micro-expressions and other non-verbal cues demands continuous learning and application. Daily practices such as mindful observation, leveraging feedback, and using technological tools can significantly accelerate this mastery. The key lies in remaining curious and motivated to improve one's communication arsenal.

In closing, I hope this book has illuminated the path to becoming a more proficient and empathetic communicator. The ability to decode non-verbal cues is more than just a skill; it's an art that bridges gaps, builds connections, and fosters understanding in an increasingly complex world. As you step forward, remember that every interaction is an opportunity to practice. Let your journey be one of perpetual growth and endless discovery.

Thank you for embarking on this journey. May the skills and insights gleaned from this book empower you to navigate the nuanced world of non-verbal communication with confidence and clarity.

Appendix A:
Additional Resources

The journey to mastering the art of micro-expressions and non-verbal communication can be complex and filled with nuances. This appendix serves as an additional resource to deepen your understanding and provide you with tools, references, and supplementary materials to further your skills.

To support your ongoing growth, we have compiled a list of books, articles, and online resources that delve deeper into topics covered in this book. Whether you're looking to refine your practice or explore new perspectives, these materials will be invaluable.

1. **Books**

    - "What Every BODY is Saying: An Ex-FBI Agent's Guide to Speed-Reading People" *by Joe Navarro*

    - "The Dictionary of Body Language: A Field Guide to Human Behavior" *by Joe Navarro*

    - "The Definitive Book of Body Language" *by Allan and Barbara Pease*

2. **Articles**

    - "Reading Between the Lines: Body Language in the Office" - *Harvard Business Review*

    - *"The Science of Facial Expressions"* - American Psychological Association

- "Micro-Expressions: Tiny Clues to Big Emotions" - *Psychology Today*

3. **Online Resources**

- **Pau Ekman Group:** An authority on micro-expressions and emotional intelligence, the site offers training tools and resources www.paulekman.com

- **Kinesics:** A comprehensive resource on non-verbal communication, including detailed articles and case studies www.kinesics.com

- **Body Language Institute:** Provides certification courses and workshops on reading body language www.bodylanguageinstitute.com

It's essential to remember that mastering non-verbal communication, particularly micro-expressions, is a continuous journey. By consistently seeking out new information and practicing your skills, you'll become more adept at interpreting the silent language of emotions.

Feel free to revisit sections of this book or explore these supplementary materials to refresh and enhance your knowledge. The power of non-verbal communication lies not just in understanding it but in applying it effectively and empathetically in diverse scenarios.

Consider this appendix as your toolkit, ready to support you whenever you need to dive deeper or revisit key concepts. Keep pushing your boundaries, and you'll find that the ability to decode non-verbal cues will transform not just your professional life, but your personal interactions as well. Embrace every opportunity for learning and growth, knowing that each step forward enhances your communication prowess.

Practice and Persistence

Learning to accurately read and interpret micro-expressions doesn't happen overnight. It requires consistent practice and a willingness to reevaluate and adjust your approach. Here are a few tips to keep the momentum going:

- **Daily Practices:** Set aside a few minutes each day to observe and interpret micro-expressions, whether through videos, real-life interactions, or structured practice sessions.

- **Feedback Sessions:** Regularly seek feedback from trusted colleagues or mentors to gauge your progress and identify areas for improvement.

- **Reflect and Adjust:** After significant interactions, take time to reflect on what you observed and how effectively you responded to non-verbal cues. Adjust your techniques based on these reflections.

As you continue on this path, remember that proficiency grows from perseverance. Embrace each learning moment and celebrate the progress you make, no matter how incremental it might seem. Your dedication to understanding and utilizing micro-expressions will undoubtedly pay off, opening doors to more profound, effective, and empathetic communication.

Happy learning and observing!

More Resources

The journey of mastering non-verbal communication is deeply intricate and rewarding. As the complexity of micro-expressions unfolds, so does the need for diverse resources to continually expand your understanding and application. This section serves as a curated collection of materials and avenues to further empower your exploration in this field.

Books and Publications

Some foundational texts provide a thorough dive into the science behind non-verbal cues. "Emotions Revealed" by Paul Ekman offers an extensive look at the subtleties of facial expressions. For an exploration of body language, "The Definitive Book of Body Language" by Allan and Barbara Pease is an excellent resource. These books serve as essential guides for those who wish to deepen their knowledge.

Journals such as "The Journal of Nonverbal Behavior" and the "Journal of Personality and Social Psychology" frequently publish cutting-edge research on micro-expressions and non-verbal communication. Subscribing to these can keep you updated on the latest studies, ensuring your knowledge remains current and robust.

Online Courses and Workshops

In the digital age, self-paced online courses offer an accessible way to sharpen your skills. Websites like Coursera and Udemy host numerous courses dedicated to emotional intelligence and body language analysis. Paul Ekman's training programs, such as "Micro Expressions Training Tool," are specifically designed to boost your ability to recognize subtle facial cues.

For a more interactive and immersive experience, consider attending workshops and seminars. Organizations like the Center for Body Language offer in-person and virtual sessions, providing hands-on practice with real-time feedback.

Podcasts and Webinars

Podcasts offer a convenient way to absorb information while on the go. "The Science of Success" and "The Nonverbal Communication Podcast" feature episodes that delve into the nuances of body language and emotional intelligence. These can serve as continuous learning channels, enriching your understanding during your daily commute or workout.

Webinars provide an opportunity to engage with experts and peers alike, fostering a community of like-minded learners. Platforms like LinkedIn Learning frequently host sessions on leadership skills, many of which cover aspects of non-verbal communication. Participating in these can help you grasp the application of theory in real-world scenarios, enhancing your practical knowledge.

Apps and Software

Technology has made it easier to practice and refine your skills in recognizing micro-expressions. Apps like "METV (Micro Expressions Training Videos)" offer visual aids and quizzes that simulate real-life scenarios. These tools are invaluable for building muscle memory and increasing your accuracy in real-time recognition.

Software tools aimed at organizational settings, such as "Noldus FaceReader," analyze recorded interactions to provide insights into emotional states. Implementing such technology in workplaces can significantly improve communication dynamics and leadership effectiveness.

Networking and Communities

Engaging with communities that focus on non-verbal communication and emotional intelligence can offer rich learning experiences. Consider joining forums like the "Body Language Institute" on Reddit or LinkedIn groups dedicated to leadership and emotional intelligence. These platforms can provide answers to specific queries and foster collaborative learning.

Attending industry conferences, such as "The Nonverbal Communication Conference" or events hosted by the Association for Psychological Science, can be invaluable. These gatherings offer a blend of learning and networking opportunities, enabling you to connect with leading experts and fellow enthusiasts.

Practice Tools and Resources

Practical application is key to mastering micro-expressions. Tools like face-to-face role-playing exercises in workshops or utilizing the feedback from recorded practice sessions can be immensely beneficial. Regularly testing yourself with these methods helps in honing the precision and speed of your recognition abilities.

Engage in reflective practices such as journaling your observations and experiences. Documenting your progress, noting successful recognitions as well as missed cues, can help you gain a sharper, self-aware perspective on your development. It provides a retrospective look at what you've learned and areas that need further improvement.

Mentors and Peers

Finding a mentor who excels in the art of non-verbal communication can be a game-changer. A mentor can provide personalized guidance, share practical insights, and offer constructive feedback. Don't underestimate the value of having someone to guide you through complex areas and encourage your growth.

Equally important are peers who share your interest. Forming a study group or a discussion circle can create a supportive environment where sharing knowledge and experiences accelerates collective learning. It fosters accountability and promotes diverse perspectives, enhancing your understanding and application of micro-expressions.

Summary

The path to decoding non-verbal cues is continuous and evolving. Diversifying your resources from books and journals to workshops, podcasts, apps, and communities ensures a holistic approach to learning. Each of these resources contributes uniquely to your skillset, fostering a comprehensive mastery over time.

Remember, the goal is not just to gather information, but to apply it in enhancing your professional and personal interactions. Embrace the journey of learning, practice consistently, and stay curious. The more resources you utilize, the better equipped you will be to navigate and decode the complex world of non-verbal communication.

Glossary of Terms

Welcome to the "Glossary of Terms." This section is designed to serve as your go-to resource for understanding the key terms and concepts you'll encounter as you dive deeper into the fascinating world of non-verbal communication and micro-expressions.

Adaptive Unconscious

The part of our brain that quickly processes incoming information, often instantly evaluating our surroundings and responding to non-verbal cues without conscious thought.

Affect Display

Visible manifestations of a person's emotions through facial expressions, body language, and vocal tone. Understanding these can help pinpoint someone's true feelings.

Baseline Behavior

The normal, habitual actions and reactions of an individual. Recognizing this is crucial for detecting deviations that might indicate stress, deception, or other significant emotional states.

Body Language

A form of non-verbal communication involving the use of physical behaviors, such as gestures, posture, and facial expressions, to convey information.

Context

The circumstances or setting surrounding a particular event or situation. In non-verbal communication, context can significantly influence the interpretation of body language and micro-expressions.

Deception Cues

Signs that may indicate someone is lying or hiding the truth. These cues can include inconsistencies between verbal statements and non-verbal behaviors.

Emotional Intelligence

The ability to recognize, understand, manage, and influence both your own emotions and those of others. High emotional intelligence enhances interpersonal communication and leadership abilities.

Empathy

The capability to deeply understand and share the feelings of another person. Through empathy, one can connect more effectively and respond more appropriately to others' emotional states.

Facial Micro-Expressions

Brief, involuntary facial expressions that occur as a direct result of an emotion experienced by an individual. These expressions are often seen when a person is attempting to conceal or repress their emotions.

Non-Verbal Communication

The exchange of messages or information without the use of words. This includes facial expressions, gestures, body language, posture, eye contact, and even the tone and pitch of voice.

Practice Techniques

Methods or exercises employed to improve the ability to recognize and interpret micro-expressions and body language. This could include facial coding, video review, or real-time observation exercises.

Real-Time Recognition

The skill of identifying and interpreting non-verbal cues and micro-expressions as they happen, crucial for effective, in-the-moment communication.

Universal Expressions

Facial expressions that are consistent across different cultures and are universally recognized, such as happiness, sadness, fear, anger, surprise, and disgust.

Verbal and Non-Verbal Synergy

The harmonious combination of spoken words and body language to enhance the effectiveness of communication. Recognizing this synergy can help convey your message more clearly and persuasively.

Use this glossary as a reference to deepen your understanding, and soon you'll find yourself more adept at reading the silent yet powerful language of micro-expressions.

www.ingramcontent.com/pod-product-compliance
Lightning Source LLC
Chambersburg PA
CBHW030340290526
45785CB00004B/1545